Baltimore Orioles 2021

A Baseball Companion

Edited by Steven Goldman and Bret Sayre

Baseball Prospectus

Craig Brown, Associate Editor
Robert Au, Harry Pavlidis and Amy Pircher, Statistics Editors

Library of Congress Cataloging-in-Publication Data:
paperback
ISBN-13: 978-1-950716-29-6

Project Credits
Cover Design: Ginny Searle
Interior Design and Production: Amy Pircher, Robert Au
Layout: Amy Pircher, Robert Au

Baseball icon courtesy of Uberux, from https://www.shareicon.net/author/uberux

Ballpark diagram courtesy of Lou Spirito/THIRTY81 Project, https://thirty81project.com/

Manufactured in the United States of America
10 9 8 7 6 5 4 3 2 1

Table of Contents

Statistical Introduction

S ports are, fundamentally, a blend of athletic endeavor and storytelling. Baseball, like any other sport, tells its stories in so many ways: in the arc of a game from the stands or a season from the box scores, in photos, or even in numbers. At Baseball Prospectus, we understand that statistics don't replace observation or any of baseball's stories, but complement everything else that makes the game so much fun.

What stats help us with is with patterns and precision, variance and value. This book can help you learn things you may not see from watching a game or hundred, whether it's the path of a career over time or the breadth of the entire MLB. We'd also never ask you to choose between our numbers and the experience of viewing a game from the cheap seats or the comfort of your home; our publication combines running the numbers with observations and wisdom from some of the brightest minds we can find. But if you *do* want to learn more about the numbers beyond what's on the backs of player jerseys, let us help explain.

Offense

We've revised our methodology for determining batting value. Long-time readers of the book will notice that we've retired True Average in favor of a new metric: Deserved Runs Created Plus (DRC+). Developed by Jonathan Judge and our stats team, this statistic measures everything a player does at the plate–reaching base, hitting for power, making outs, and moving runners over–and puts it on a scale where 100 equals league-average performance. A DRC+ of 150 is terrific, a DRC+ of 100 is average and a DRC+ of 75 means you better be an excellent defender.

DRC+ also does a better job than any of our previous metrics in taking contextual factors into account. The model adjusts for how the park affects performance, but also for things like the talent of the opposing pitcher, value of different types of batted-ball events, league, temperature and other factors. It's able to describe a player's expected offensive contribution than any other statistic we've found over the years, and also does a better job of predicting future performance as well.

The other aspect of run-scoring is baserunning, which we quantify using Baserunning Runs. BRR not only records the value of stolen bases (or getting caught in the act), but also accounts for all the stuff that doesn't show up on the back of a baseball card: a runner's ability to go first to third on a single, or advance on a fly ball.

Defense

Where offensive value is *relatively* easy to identify and understand, defensive value is … not. Over the past dozen years, the sabermetric community has focused mostly on stats based on zone data: a real-live human person records the type of batted ball and estimated landing location, and models are created that give expected outs. From there, you can compare fielders' actual outs to those expected ones. Simple, right?

Unfortunately, zone data has two major issues. First, zone data is recorded by commercial data providers who keep the raw data private unless you pay for it. (All the statistics we build in this book and on our website use public data as inputs.) That hurts our ability to test assumptions or duplicate results. Second, over the years it has become apparent that there's quite a bit of "noise" in zone-based fielding analysis. Sometimes the conclusions drawn from zone data don't hold up to scrutiny, and sometimes the different data provided by different providers don't look anything alike, giving wildly different results. Sometimes the hard-working professional stringers or scorers might unknowingly inflict unconscious bias into the mix: for example good fielders will often be credited with more expected outs despite the data, and ballparks with high press boxes tend to score more line drives than ones with a lower press box.

Enter our Fielding Runs Above Average (FRAA). For most positions, FRAA is built from play-by-play data, which allows us to avoid the subjectivity found in many other fielding metrics. The idea is this: count how many fielding plays are made by a given player and compare that to expected plays for an average fielder at their position (based on pitcher ground ball tendencies and batter handedness). Then we adjust for park and base-out situations.

When it comes to catchers, our methodology is a little different thanks to the laundry list of responsibilities they're tasked with beyond just, well, catching and throwing the ball. By now you've probably heard about "framing" or the art of making umpires more likely to call balls outside the strike zone for strikes. To put this into one tidy number, we incorporate pitch tracking data (for the years it exists) and adjust for important factors like pitcher, umpire, batter and home-field advantage using a mixed-model approach. This grants us a number for how many strikes the catcher is personally adding to (or subtracting from) his pitchers' performance … which we then convert to runs added or lost using linear weights.

Framing is one of the biggest parts of determining catcher value, but we also take into account blocking balls from going past, whether a scorer deems it a passed ball or a wild pitch. We use a similar approach—one that really benefits from the pitch tracking data that tells us what ends up in the dirt and what doesn't. We also include a catcher's ability to prevent stolen bases and how well they field balls in play, and *finally* we come up with our FRAA for catchers.

Pitching

Both pitching and fielding make up the half of baseball that isn't run scoring: run prevention. Separating pitching from fielding is a tough task, and most recent pitching analysis has branched off from Voros McCracken's famous (and controversial) statement, "There is little if any difference among major-league pitchers in their ability to prevent hits on balls hit in the field of play." The research of the analytic community has validated this to some extent, and there are a host of "defense-independent" pitching measures that have been developed to try and extract the effect of the defense behind a hurler from the pitcher's work.

Our solution to this quandary is Deserved Run Average (DRA), our core pitching metric. DRA seeks to evaluate a pitcher's performance, much like earned run average (ERA), the tried-and-true pitching stat you've seen on every baseball broadcast or box score from the past century, but it's very different. To start, DRA takes an event-by-event look at what the pitchers does, and adjusts the value of that event based on different environmental factors like park, batter, catcher, umpire, base-out situation, run differential, inning, defense, home field advantage, pitcher role and temperature. That mixed model gives us a pitcher's expected contribution, similar to what we do for our DRC+ model for hitters and FRAA model for catchers. (Oh, and we also consider the pitcher's effect on basestealing and on balls getting past the catcher.)

DRA is set to the scale of runs allowed per nine innings (RA9) instead of ERA, which makes DRA's scale slightly higher than ERA's. Because of this, for ease of use, we're supplying DRA-, which is much easier for the reader to parse. As with DRC+, DRA- is an "index" stat, meaning instead of using some arbitrary and shifting number to denote what's "good," average is always 100. The reason that it uses a minus rather than a plus is because like ERA, a lower number is better. Therefore a 75 DRA- describes a performance 25 percent better than average, whereas a 150 DRA- means that either a pitcher is getting extremely lucky with their results, or getting ready to try a new pitch.

Since the last time you picked up an edition of this book, we've also made a few minor changes to DRA to make it better. Recent research into "tunneling"—the act of throwing consecutive pitches that appear similar from a batter's point of view until after the swing decision point–data has given us a new contextual factor to account for in DRA: plate distance. This refers to the distance between successive pitches as they approach the plate, and while it has a smaller effect than factors like velocity or whiff rate, it still can help explain pitcher strikeout rate in our model.

Recently Added Descriptive Statistics

Returning to our 2021 edition of the book are a few figures which recently appeared. These numbers may be a little bit more familiar to those of you who have spent some time investigating baseball statistics.

Fastball Percentage

Our fastball percentage (FA%) statistic measures how frequently a pitcher throws a pitch classified as a "fastball," measured as a percentage of overall pitches thrown. We qualify three types of fastballs:

1. The traditional four-seam fastball;
2. The two-seam fastball or sinker;
3. "Hard cutters," which are pitches that have the movement profile of a cut fastball and are used as the pitcher's primary offering or in place of a more traditional fastball.

For example, a pitcher with a FA% of 67 throws any combination of these three pitches about two-thirds of the time.

Whiff Rate

Everybody loves a swing and a miss, and whiff rate (Whiff%) measures how frequently pitchers induce a swinging strike. To calculate Whiff%, we add up all the pitches thrown that ended with a swinging strike, then divide that number by a pitcher's total pitches thrown. Most often, high whiff rates correlate with high strikeout rates (and overall effective pitcher performance).

Called Strike Probability

Called Strike Probability (CSP) is a number that represents the likelihood that all of a pitcher's pitches will be called a strike while controlling for location, pitcher and batter handedness, umpire and count. Here's how it works: on each pitch, our model determines how many times (out of 100) that a similar pitch was called for a strike given those factors mentioned above, and when normalized for each batter's strike zone. Then we average the CSP for all pitches thrown by a pitcher in a season, and that gives us the yearly CSP percentage you see in the stats boxes.

As you might imagine, pitchers with a higher CSP are more likely to work in the zone, where pitchers with a lower CSP are likely locating their pitches outside the normal strike zone, for better or for worse.

Projections

Many of you aren't turning to this book just for a look at what a player has done, but for a look at what a player is going to do: the PECOTA projections. PECOTA, initially developed by Nate Silver (who has moved on to greater fame as a political analyst), consists of three parts:

1. Major-league equivalencies, which use minor-league statistics to project how a player will perform in the major leagues;
2. Baseline forecasts, which use weighted averages and regression to the mean to estimate a player's current true talent level; and
3. Aging curves, which uses the career paths of comparable players to estimate how a player's statistics are likely to change over time.

With all those important things covered, let's take a look at what's in the book this year.

Team Prospectus

Most of this book is composed of team chapters, with one for each of the 30 major-league franchises. On the first page of each chapter, you'll see a box that contains some of the key statistics for each team as well as a very inviting stadium diagram.

We start with the team name, their unadjusted 2020 win-loss record, and their divisional ranking. Beneath that are a host of other team statistics. **Pythag** presents an adjusted 2020 winning percentage, calculated by taking runs scored per game (**RS/G**) and runs allowed per game (**RA/G**) for the team, and running them through a version of Bill James' Pythagorean formula that was refined and improved by David Smyth and Brandon Heipp. (The formula is called "Pythagenpat," which is equally fun to type and to say.)

Next up is **DRC+**, described earlier, to indicate the overall hitting ability of the team either above or below league-average. Run prevention on the pitching side is covered by **DRA** (also mentioned earlier) and another metric: Fielding Independent Pitching (**FIP**), which calculates another ERA-like statistic based on strikeouts, walks, and home runs recorded. Defensive Efficiency Rating (**DER**) tells us the percentage of balls in play turned into outs for the team, and is a quick fielding shorthand that rounds out run prevention.

After that, we have several measures related to roster composition, as opposed to on-field performance. **B-Age** and **P-Age** tell us the average age of a team's batters and pitchers, respectively. **Payroll** is the combined team payroll for all on-field players, and Doug Pappas' Marginal Dollars per Marginal Win (**M$/MW**) tells us how much money a team spent to earn production above replacement level.

Next to each of these stats, we've listed each team's MLB rank in that category from first to 30th. In this, first always indicates a positive outcome and 30th a negative outcome, except in the case of salary—first is highest.

After the franchise statistics, we share a few items about the team's home ballpark. There's the aforementioned diagram of the park's dimensions (including distances to the outfield wall), a graphic showing the height of the wall from the left-field pole to the right-field pole, and a table showing three-year park factors for the stadium. The park factors are displayed as indexes where 100 is average, 110 means that the park inflates the statistic in question by 10 percent, and 90 means that the park deflates the statistic in question by 10 percent.

On the second page of each team chapter, you'll find three graphs. The first is **Payroll History** and helps you see how the team's payroll has compared to the MLB and divisional average payrolls over time. Payroll figures are current as of January 1, 2021; with so many free agents still unsigned as of this writing, the final 2021 figure will likely be significantly different for many teams. (In the meantime, you can always find the most current data at Baseball Prospectus' Cot's Baseball Contracts page.)

The second graph is **Future Commitments** and helps you see the team's future outlays, if any.

The third graph is **Farm System Ranking** and displays how the Baseball Prospectus prospect team has ranked the organization's farm system since 2007.

After the graphs, we have a **Personnel** section that lists many of the important decision-makers and upper-level field and operations staff members for the franchise, as well as any former Baseball Prospectus staff members who are currently part of the organization. (In very rare circumstances, someone might be on both lists!)

Position Players

After all that information and a thoughtful bylined essay covering each team, we present our player comments. These are also bylined, but due to frequent franchise shifts during the offseason, our bylines are more a rough guide than a perfect accounting of who wrote what.

Each player is listed with the major-league team that employed him as of early January 2021. If a player changed teams after that point via free agency, trade, or any other method, you'll be able to find them in the chapter for their previous squad.

As an example, take a look at the player comment for Padres shortstop Fernando Tatis Jr.: the stat block that accompanies his written comment is at the top of this page. First we cover biographical information (age is as of June 30, 2021) before moving onto the stats themselves. Our statistic columns include standard identifying information like **YEAR**, **TEAM**, **LVL** (level of affiliated play) and **AGE** before getting into the numbers. Next, we provide raw, untranslated

Fernando Tatis Jr. SS

Born: 01/02/99   Age: 22   Bats: R   Throws: R
Height: 6'3"   Weight: 217   Origin: International Free Agent, 2015

YEAR	TEAM	LVL	AGE	PA	R	2B	3B	HR	RBI	BB	K	SB	CS	AVG/OBP/SLG
2018	SA	AA	19	394	77	22	4	16	43	33	109	16	5	.286/.355/.507
2019	SD	MLB	20	372	61	13	6	22	53	30	110	16	6	.317/.379/.590
2020	SD	MLB	21	257	50	11	2	17	45	27	61	11	3	.277/.366/.571
2021 FS	SD	MLB	22	600	95	24	4	31	81	50	165	17	8	.263/.331/.499
2021 DC	SD	MLB	22	628	100	25	4	32	85	53	173	19	8	.263/.331/.499

Comparables: Darryl Strawberry, Bo Bichette, Ronald Acuña Jr.

YEAR	TEAM	LVL	AGE	PA	DRC+	BABIP	BRR	FRAA	WARP
2018	SA	AA	19	394	136	.370	3.0	SS(83): -1.9	2.4
2019	SD	MLB	20	372	118	.410	7.1	SS(83): 0.9	3.4
2020	SD	MLB	21	257	126	.306	0.7	SS(57): -5.5	0.9
2021 FS	SD	MLB	22	600	126	.318	1.7	SS -1	3.9
2021 DC	SD	MLB	22	628	126	.318	1.8	SS -1	4.0

numbers like you might find on the back of your dad's baseball cards: **PA** (plate appearances), **R** (runs), **2B** (doubles), **3B** (triples), **HR** (home runs), **RBI** (runs batted in), **BB** (walks), **K** (strikeouts), **SB** (stolen bases) and **CS** (caught stealing).

Following the basic stats is **Whiff%** (whiff rate), which denotes how often, when a batter swings, he fails to make contact with the ball. Another way to think of this number is an inverse of a hitter's contact rate.

Next, we have unadjusted "slash" statistics: **AVG** (batting average), **OBP** (on-base percentage) and **SLG** (slugging percentage). Following the slash line is **DRC+** (Deserved Runs Created Plus), which we described earlier as total offensive expected contribution compared to the league average.

BABIP (batting average on balls in play) tells us how often a ball in play fell for a hit, and can help us identify whether a batter may have been lucky or not ... but note that high BABIPs also tend to follow the great hitters of our time, as well as speedy singles hitters who put the ball on the ground.

The next item is **BRR** (Baserunning Runs), which covers all of a player's baserunning accomplishments including (but not limited to) swiped bags and failed attempts. Next is **FRAA** (Fielding Runs Above Average), which also includes the number of games previously played at each position noted in parentheses. Multi-position players have only their two most frequent positions listed here, but their total FRAA number reflects all positions played.

Our last column here is **WARP** (Wins Above Replacement Player). WARP estimates the total value of a player, which means for hitters it takes into account hitting runs above average (calculated using the DRC+ model), BRR and FRAA. Then, it makes an adjustment for positions played and gives the player a credit for plate appearances based upon the difference between "replacement level"—which is derived from the quality of players added to a team's roster after the start of the season–and the league average.

The final line just below the stats box is **PECOTA** data, which is discussed further in a following section.

Catchers

Catchers are a special breed, and thus they have earned their own separate box which displays some of the defensive metrics that we've built just for them. As an example, let's check out Yasmani Grandal.

YEAR	TEAM	P. COUNT	FRM RUNS	BLK RUNS	THRW RUNS	TOT RUNS
2018	LAD	16816	15.7	0.8	0.1	16.5
2019	MIL	18740	19.4	1.8	-0.1	21.1
2020	CHW	4830	3.7	0.3	-0.2	3.8
2021	CHW	14430	16.7	-0.6	1.0	17.1
2021	CHW	14430	16.7	0.4	1.0	18.0

The **YEAR** and **TEAM** columns match what you'd find in the other stat box. **P. COUNT** indicates the number of pitches thrown while the catcher was behind the plate, including swinging strikes, fouls and balls in play. **FRM RUNS** is the total run value the catcher provided (or cost) his team by influencing the umpire to call strikes where other catchers did not. **BLK RUNS** expresses the total run value above or below average for the catcher's ability to prevent wild pitches and passed balls. **THRW RUNS** is calculated using a similar model as the previous two statistics, and it measures a catcher's ability to throw out basestealers but also to dissuade them from testing his arm in the first place. It takes into account factors like the pitcher (including his delivery and pickoff move) and baserunner (who could be as fast as Billy Hamilton or as slow as Yonder Alonso). **TOT RUNS** is the sum of all of the previous three statistics.

Pitchers

Let's give our pitchers a turn, using 2020 AL Cy Young winner Shane Bieber as our example. Take a look at his stat block: the first line and the **YEAR**, **TEAM**, **LVL** and **AGE** columns are the same as in the position player example earlier.

Here too, we have a series of columns that display raw, unadjusted statistics compiled by the pitcher over the course of a season: **W** (wins), **L** (losses), **SV** (saves), **G** (games pitched), **GS** (games started), **IP** (innings pitched), **H** (hits allowed) and **HR** (home runs allowed). Next we have two statistics that are rates: **BB/9** (walks per nine innings) and **K/9** (strikeouts per nine innings), before returning to the unadjusted K (strikeouts).

Next up is **GB%** (ground ball percentage), which is the percentage of all batted balls that were hit on the ground, including both outs and hits. Remember, this is based on observational data and subject to human error, so please approach this with a healthy dose of skepticism.

BABIP (batting average on balls in play) is calculated using the same methodology as it is for position players, but it often tells us more about a pitcher than it does a hitter. With pitchers, a high BABIP is often due to poor defense or bad luck, and can often be an indicator of potential rebound, and a low BABIP may be cause to expect performance regression. (A typical league-average BABIP is close to .290-.300.)

The metrics **WHIP** (walks plus hits per inning pitched) and **ERA** (earned run average) are old standbys: WHIP measures walks and hits allowed on a per-inning basis, while ERA measures earned runs on a nine-inning basis. Neither of these stats are translated or adjusted.

DRA- (Deserved Run Average) was described at length earlier, and measures how the pitcher "deserved" to perform compared to other pitchers. Please note that since we lack all the data points that would make for a "real" DRA for minor-league events, the DRA- displayed for minor league partial-seasons is based off of different data. (That data is a modified version of our cFIP metric, which you can find more information about on our website.)

Shane Bieber   RHP

Born: 05/31/95   Age: 26   Bats: R   Throws: R
Height: 6'3"   Weight: 200   Origin: Round 4, 2016 Draft (#122 overall)

YEAR	TEAM	LVL	AGE	W	L	SV	G	GS	IP	H	HR	BB/9	K/9	K	GB%	BABIP
2018	AKR	AA	23	3	0	0	5	5	31	26	1	0.3	8.7	30	47.3%	.278
2018	COL	AAA	23	3	1	0	8	8	48²	30	3	1.1	8.7	47	52.0%	.227
2018	CLE	MLB	23	11	5	0	20	19	114²	130	13	1.8	9.3	118	46.2%	.356
2019	CLE	MLB	24	15	8	0	34	33	214¹	186	31	1.7	10.9	259	44.4%	.298
2020	CLE	MLB	25	8	1	0	12	12	77¹	46	7	2.4	14.2	122	48.4%	.267
2021 FS	CLE	MLB	26	10	6	0	26	26	150	121	18	2.1	11.7	195	45.5%	.297
2021 DC	CLE	MLB	26	14	7	0	30	30	196.7	159	24	2.1	11.7	257	45.5%	.297

Comparables: Luis Severino, Danny Salazar, Joe Musgrove

YEAR	TEAM	LVL	AGE	WHIP	ERA	DRA-	WARP	MPH	FB%	WHF	CSP
2018	AKR	AA	23	0.87	1.16	61	0.9				
2018	COL	AAA	23	0.74	1.66	69	1.2				
2018	CLE	MLB	23	1.33	4.55	74	2.6	94.7	57.4%	26.2%	
2019	CLE	MLB	24	1.05	3.28	75	4.9	94.4	45.8%	30.8%	
2020	CLE	MLB	25	0.87	1.63	53	2.6	95.3	53.6%	40.7%	
2021 FS	CLE	MLB	26	1.04	2.44	64	4.4	94.7	50.0%	33.2%	44.2%
2021 DC	CLE	MLB	26	1.04	2.44	64	5.8	94.7	50.0%	33.2%	44.2%

Just like with hitters, **WARP** (Wins Above Replacement Player) is a total value metric that puts pitchers of all stripes on the same scale as position players. We use DRA as the primary input for our calculation of WARP. You might notice that relief pitchers (due to their limited innings) may have a lower WARP than you were expecting or than you might see in other WARP-like metrics. WARP does not take leverage into account, just the actions a pitcher performs and the expected value of those actions ... which ends up judging high-leverage relief pitchers differently than you might imagine given their prestige and market value.

MPH gives you the pitcher's 95th percentile velocity for the noted season, in order to give you an idea of what the *peak* fastball velocity a pitcher possesses. Since this comes from our pitch-tracking data, it is not publicly available for minor-league pitchers.

Finally, we display the three new pitching metrics we described earlier. **FB%** (fastball percentage) gives you the percentage of fastballs thrown out of all pitches. **WHF** (whiff rate) tells you the percentage of swinging strikes induced out of all pitches. **CSP** (called strike probability) expresses the likelihood of all pitches thrown to result in a called strike, after controlling for factors like handedness, umpire, pitch type, count and location.

PECOTA

All players have PECOTA projections for 2021, as well as a set of other numbers that describe the performance of comparable players according to PECOTA. All projections for 2021 are for the player at the date we went to press in early January and are projected into the league and park context as indicated by the team abbreviation. (Note that players at very low levels of the minors are too unpredictable to assess using these numbers.) All PECOTA projected statistics represent a player's projected major-league performance.

How we're doing that is a little different this season. There are really two different values that go into the final stat line that you see for PECOTA: How a player performs, and how much playing time he'll be given to perform it. In the past we've estimated playing time based on each team's roster and depth charts, and we'll continue to do that. These projections are denoted as **2021 DC**.

But in many cases, a player won't be projected for major-league playing time; most of the time this is because they aren't projected to be major-league players at all, but still developing as prospects. Or perhaps a player will provide Triple-A depth, only to have an opportunity open up because of injury. For these purposes, we're also supplying a second projection, labeled **2021 FS**, or full season. This is what we would project the player to provide in 600 plate appearances or 150 innings pitched.

Below the projections are the player's three highest-scoring comparable players as determined by PECOTA. All comparables represent a snapshot of how the listed player was performing at the same age as the current player, so if a

23-year-old pitcher is compared to Bartolo Colón, he's actually being compared to a 23-year-old Colón, not the version that pitched for the Rangers in 2018, nor to Colón's career as a whole.

A few points about pitcher projections. First, we aren't yet projecting peak velocity, so that column will be blank in the PECOTA lines. Second, projecting DRA is trickier than evaluating past performance, because it is unclear how deserving each pitcher will be of his anticipated outcomes. However, we know that another DRA-related statistic–contextual FIP or cFIP-estimates future run scoring very well. So for PECOTA, the projected DRA- figures you see are based on the past cFIPs generated by the pitcher and comparable players over time, along with the other factors described above.

If you're familiar with PECOTA, then you'll have noticed that the projection system often appears bullish on players coming off a bad year and bearish on players coming off a good year. (This is because the system weights several previous seasons, not just the most recent one.) In addition, we publish the 50th percentile projections for each player–which is smack in the middle of the range of projected production—which tends to mean PECOTA stat lines don't often have extreme results like 40 home runs or 250 strikeouts in a given season. In essence, PECOTA doesn't project very many extreme seasons.

Managers

After all those wonderful team chapters, we've got statistics for each big-league manager, all of whom are organized by alphabetical order. Here you'll find a block including an extraordinary amount of information collected from each manager's entire career. For more information on the acronyms and what they mean, please visit the Glossary at www.baseballprospectus.com.

There is one important metric that we'd like to call attention to, and you'll find it next to each manager's name: **wRM+** (weighted reliever management plus). Developed by Rob Arthur and Rian Watt, wRM+ investigates how good a manager is at using their best relievers during the moments of highest leverage, using both our proprietary DRA metric as well as Leverage Index. wRM+ is scaled to a league average of 100, and a wRM+ of 105 indicates that relievers were used approximately five percent "better" than average. On the other hand, a wRM+ of 95 would tell us the team used its relievers five percent "worse" than the average team.

While wRM+ does not have an extremely strong correlation with a manager, it is statistically significant; this means that a manager is not *entirely* responsible for a team's wRM+, but does have some effect on that number.

Part 1: Team Analysis

Part I: Team Analysis

Performance Graphs

Payroll History (in millions)

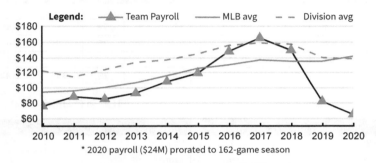

* 2020 payroll ($24M) prorated to 162-game season

Future Commitments (in millions)

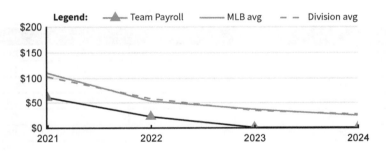

Farm System Ranking

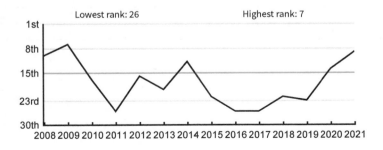

2020 Team Performance

ACTUAL STANDINGS

Team	W	L	Pct
TB	40	20	0.667
NYY	33	27	0.550
TOR	32	28	0.533
BAL	**25**	**35**	**0.417**
BOS	24	36	0.400

dWIN% STANDINGS

Team	W	L	Pct
NYY	33	27	0.560
TB	29	31	0.495
BOS	25	35	0.429
TOR	25	35	0.425
BAL	**25**	**35**	**0.420**

TOP HITTERS

Player	WARP
Anthony Santander	1.4
Pat Valaika	0.7
DJ Stewart	0.7

TOP PITCHERS

Player	WARP
Paul Fry	0.6
Tanner Scott	0.5
Alex Cobb	0.5

VITAL STATISTICS

Statistic Name	Value	Rank
Pythagenpat	.466	19th
dWin%	.420	23rd
Runs Scored per Game	4.57	17th
Runs Allowed per Game	4.90	16th
Deserved Runs Created Plus	97	17th
Deserved Run Average Minus	103	20th
Fielding Independent Pitching	4.79	20th
Defensive Efficiency Rating	.705	12th
Batter Age	26.8	2nd
Pitcher Age	28.6	19th
Payroll	$24.0M	29th
Marginal $ per Marginal Win	$0.9M	2nd

2021 Team Projections

PROJECTED STANDINGS

Team	W	L	Pct	+/-
NYY	99.5	62.5	0.614	10
The starting rotation was loaded with risk even before Corey Kluber and Jameson Taillon became members. At least D.J. LeMahieu should keep the lineup humming.				
TB	86.0	76.0	0.531	-22
The defending AL champions didn't really spend their winter defending anything.				
TOR	84.4	77.6	0.521	-2
They stopped a starting pitcher short of credibly claiming favorite status, but adding George Springer gives them one of the junior circuit's most lethal lineups.				
BOS	79.3	82.7	0.490	14
There's a faint flavor of their 2012-13 offseason to what Boston did this winter, and look how that year turned out.				
BAL	**66.1**	**95.9**	**0.408**	**-1**
Mike Elias was forthright about his disinterest in winning in the short term. His winter proved he was serious.				

TOP PROJECTED HITTERS

Player	WARP
Austin Hays	2.1
Anthony Santander	1.6
Trey Mancini	1.4

TOP PROJECTED PITCHERS

Player	WARP
John Means	2.2
Dean Kremer	1.6
Shawn Armstrong	0.9

FARM SYSTEM REPORT

Top Prospect	Number of Top 101 Prospects
Adley Rutschman, #2	5

KEY DEDUCTIONS

Player	WARP
José Iglesias	1.2
Alex Cobb	0.8

KEY ADDITIONS

Player	WARP
Freddy Galvis	0.7
Yolmer Sánchez	0.7
Fernando Abad	0.4

Team Personnel

Executive Vice President and General Manager
Mike Elias

Vice President & Assistant General Manager, Analytics
Sig Mejdal

Director, Baseball Development
Eve Rosenbaum

Director, Baseball Administration
Kevin Buck

Director, Player Development
Matt Blood

Manager
Brandon Hyde

BP Alumni
Kevin Carter

Oriole Park at Camden Yards Stats

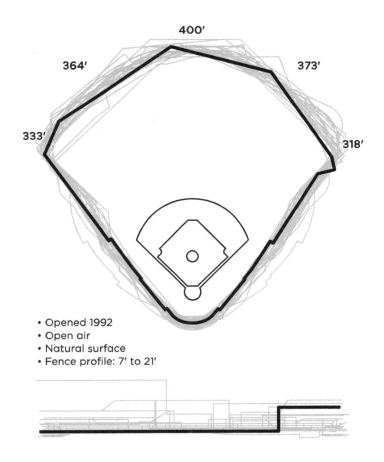

364'
400'
373'
333'
318'

- Opened 1992
- Open air
- Natural surface
- Fence profile: 7' to 21'

Three-Year Park Factors

Runs	Runs/RH	Runs/LH	HR/RH	HR/LH
101	102	100	111	106

Orioles Team Analysis

Fans of a certain age can probably remember a time where the Orioles were Major League Baseball's model franchise. (That person is not me; not because I'm TikTok young, but because I'm not Methodist-church-bowling-club old.) From 1966 through 1983, they won three titles, six pennants and finished over .500 every single year. They achieved the idyllic, sustained run of contention that has become en vogue for every team, ranging from the Rays to the Hal Steinbrenner-owned Yankees, where not an excess dollar is spent on personnel—and, preferably, considerably less than that.

The more recent editions of the Orioles are the league's model franchise in a different sense—rather than being trendsetters or trailblazers, they're copycatters following the same template every franchise has since Jeff Luhnow launched the Houston Astros into the championship echelon. There's nothing particularly new or original in the Luhnowian blueprint: the first few years entail trading veterans for prospects, losing games, collecting high draft picks—and then, eventually, winning. And, if you don't start winning, your prospects have become veterans, so you can just repeat the cycle.

The five-year plan has become the accepted term for rebuilding, to the point of appearing non-negotiable . What the Orioles have done is just the same thing as the Astros (and other imitators since), only harder—they've stripped down further, cutting closer to the bone than any franchise before them. It's not just the beloved veterans who have been sacrificed for progress; every spot on the roster, down to the arbitration-eligible infield, has been robbed of any hint of copper. Rebuilding has *always* been an ugly business; the Orioles are tearing the veil, right before placing the veil on waivers.

⚾   ⚾   ⚾

After cratering in the form of an abysmal 47-win season in 2018, the Orioles axed Dan Duquette, the architect of three playoff teams. In his place, Baltimore hired Mike Elias from Houston, where he had witnessed Luhnow stripmining the big-league roster only to do a bang, bang, bang-up job of remaking the Astros into a perennial title contender.

By the time Elias took the helm, there wasn't much left to raze. Manny Machado, the best player fielded by the previous regime, had already been traded to the Dodgers. Closer Zack Britton had been shipped to the Yankees.

Adam Jones, who had exercised his no-trade clause to remain in town, was a free agent, but Elias showed little interest in retaining the fan favorite as he approached the twilight of his starry career. Too many of the vets who remained, like first baseman Chris Davis and righty Alex Cobb, were ineffective major leaguers making tens of millions more than anyone wanted to pay them.

The Orioles might be further along in their rebuild had they received any surefire big-league pieces in return. Of the eight combined players they added during their 2018 firesale, only Dillon Tate has shown promise at the big-league level. (Outfielder Yusniel Diaz and pitcher Dean Kremer haven't received much of an opportunity yet.) That wasn't Elias' fault. Predictably, he cleared out everything from Duquette's tenure, from competitive payrolls to dozens of front office staff.

All that remains from 2018 was the org's uncanny ability to get finessed by their trade partners, giving up players they failed to evaluate or develop. Though it sounds absurd, Elias entered spring 2019 with two players in the organization who would go on to finish in the top-10 in 2020 Cy Young and Most Valuable Player Award voting, in right-hander Dylan Bundy and outfielder Mike Yastrzemski. He traded each without getting a substantive return.

Bundy became the latest face—displacing Jake Arrieta and Kevin Gausman—of the *Pitchers of Baltimore vs. The Orioles* class action lawsuit by making good on his promise. He turned around his mediocre-to-date career by flourishing with an Angels organization that isn't known for being a pitching factory. Yastrzemski, meanwhile, didn't unlock the recessive gene that made his grandfather a Hall of Famer until he arrived in San Francisco; nü-Yaz has since hit .281/.357/.535 with 31 home runs in 161 games. If only he put up those numbers while wearing the *other* orange and black, the Orioles might have a budding star on their hands. If only they'd given him some playing time to find out what they had.

Most of Elias' problems are ones that he inherited, yes, but he's yet to fix them. Look, he and Sig Mejdal and company were the ones who bought all those Edgertronic cameras and authored all those SQL scripts—getting talented players in the organization to become their best selves is part of their mandate. Their inability to do so goes hand in hand with self-evaluation (or lack thereof) and getting fleeced in trades. There's a feedback loop at play: the players Baltimore trades are bad because they were trained by Baltimore, and the players they receive are bad because they are now subject to the cruel punishment of being trained by Baltimore. If you can't make your own players good, how can you expect to get anything from them? And, further, how can the Astros plan work if the prospects you draft and acquire are never likely to live up to their potential with your organization?

Optimizing the return on players has been an issue for Elias. The last big trade he made in 2019—dumping Jonathan Villar, who they intended to non-tender, on the Marlins for his final year of team control—saw the Orioles recoup a lesser prospect than what the Marlins were able to convert Villar into at the following deadline … and that was with him having a miserable season at the plate.

What separates these Orioles from other rebuilding teams—even those fully attuned to the guiding force that is The Process—is their indifference to both the literal victories and the symbolic. Most front offices would have touted Villar—or, more recently—José Iglesias, Renato Núñez and Hanser Alberto, a trio that contributed nearly three Wins Above Replacement in 2020 after being added for scraps, as their vision's proof of concept. Not these Orioles, not under Elias.

Iglesias was Baltimore's top hitter, slashing .373/.400/.556 while providing good defense at shortstop. The Orioles waited until the last minute to exercise his affordable club option, however, and then spun him off to the Angels for two prospects who were not considered among the best in a fairly weak system—albeit one that the Orioles seemingly favor more than the consensus. Núñez and Alberto somehow received even less of a gracious sendoff. They were both non-tendered at season's end—that despite Núñez homering 50 times in 263 career games with Baltimore, and the versatile Alberto running his two-year line with the Orioles to .299/.322/.413.

The Orioles could have kept all three players at a reasonable cost: optimistic arbitration projections for Núñez and Alberto had the trio making less than $12 million combined. Yet Elias deemed that to be too much to pay per win. This isn't a bug of The Process so much as it is a feature: you may not win games, but you will keep your job by saving your owner money.

⚾   ⚾   ⚾

The game has changed since the Earl Weaver's glory days. Front offices have Cerebro-level access to data and sophisticated tools with which to synthesize information (in part due to publications like this one). Because there's less mystery about what makes a baseball player good or bad, there's more rational (and supposedly accurate) appraisals of the on-field value said player brings to your team. It's nerdy as hell. But, no shade—math is power. After all, it was math (granted, the back-of-the-napkin kind) that made Weaver's three-run homer and platoon-heavy strategies so effective in their time.

The great paradox of the modern game is that the infusion of science and math has disguised its own dark age, where anticompetiveness has run amok. The undergirding philosophy behind how such data is interpreted and wielded favors keeping as much money as possible in the pocket of team owners, as do the rules (formal or otherwise) for accumulating baseball talent. Such an imbalance provides an acceptable pretext for trading, say, Mookie Betts, of whom there is only one, for a handful of players who cannot hit, field, throw or run as well as

Mookie, but, to their credit, are currently exempt from federal wage law. Why not, when the last shall be first in payroll efficiency, and the weak inherit the Earth's best young players in the draft?

Of course, what's less talked about in regards to tanking is that the more socially acceptable it becomes—and it's en vogue at present—the less effective it is as a strategy. That's how the Orioles posted their second-worst record ever and yet they still finished second in the Spencer Torkelson sweepstakes. At least there's always a consolation prize: Even those teams who don't fail hard enough save money.

Without tracing the path from Adam Smith to Charlie Finley to Stuart Sternberg, none of this is new, and it may not even be more nefarious. Just more deft. The language of choice used to convey these strategies is no longer seasoned in jargon picked up on backfields, but in corporate boardrooms. Everything is about probabilistic analysis; optionality; or sustainability, a word whose meaning is in the eyes of whoever reads it last, usually from a sleek Powerpoint slide.

What I'm saying is this: Orioles are not alone, and there are more than enough bird brains to go around.

⚾   ⚾   ⚾

Unless you're Jake Mintz—an O's fan who would gladly elbow Jeffrey Maier in the solar plexus if it meant redeeming the past—you didn't need PECOTA to predict that the 2020 Orioles weren't making the playoffs. The Orioles were projected to go 22-38 over the pandemic-shortened season. Prorated over a normal season, that's a 58- or 59-win pace—abysmal by any standards except their own. But then, a funny thing happened: the Orioles won some games, going 12-8 out of the gate, succeeding against the Red Sox and the Nationals, the last two champions.

Anthony Santander, one of the young guys in their Maybe Talented Enough to Trade in Arbitration bucket, posted a 139 DRC+—a product of cutting down on strikeouts by leaning into his youthful aggression in the strike zone. Alex Cobb regained some of his old luster, and the rest of the pitching staff—a medley of create-a-players to the average fan—were ordinarily mediocre (4.51 ERA) instead of Gleyber Torres' personal batting practice tossers. Chris Davis even joined the party, and drove in a run.

A 12-8 start doesn't have incredible diagnostic merit. But when the season is 60 games long, who cares? That's doubly so when the usual postseason size was boosted from 10 to 16 teams, an attempt to add extra TV revenue to mitigate the loss of gate receipts. Contention is a social construct.

Besides, those 12 wins were in the bank, and not even the Orioles could negatively regress their win total. They tried their best, however, playing themselves down to a 14-19 record entering the August 31 trade deadline. And so, they did what they always do, even if they don't particularly do it well. They threw their stuff on a tarp on the lawn, and they sold.

The odds for maintaining or augmenting weren't in their favor, for understandable reasons. The on-paper talent was bad, and ominously playing to their projections. Though they were in closer position to a playoff seed than expected, they still would have had to leapfrog at least two of the three teams immediately ahead of them: the Tigers, Blue Jays and Twins. It would be all too easy to point at the spreadsheets and shrug helplessly.

However, by the same points or their direct corollary, 2020 was the best opportunity to try something. Consider that the market for decent players who could mitigate an impending regression was in their favor—the low cost the Jays, a team they were in direct competition with (well, you know ... sorta) for a playoff spot rented Taijuan Walker, Robbie Ray and Villar.There was minimal cost to getting better, with little chance in significantly harming their long-term outlook. The Orioles should know this intimately because they were the sellers in a buyer's market, shipping off relievers Mychal Givens and Miguel Castro in separate deals to Colorado and the Mets, and sending Opening Day starter—really; you could look it up—Tommy Milone to the Braves.

Though all three were performing reasonably well for Baltimore, none were world-beaters. The Castro trade was specifically odd all the same, given that, at least from one perspective, he was the kind of young, developing cost-controlled talent the Orioles are and were supposed to be adding to their ranks. Just 25 and blessed with a live arm and a huge jump in strikeout rate, he's the type of player that rebuilding teams generally collect in payment. In return for Castro, they received Kevin Smith, a player believed to be a future number five starter if everything breaks right.

Worse, 2020, in all its chaos, provided case studies of the present reward of a bad team going for it, and the risk of shying away. Look at the Marlins. Miami was not only competing with the Orioles for the top pick in the 2019 draft, they had various factors working against their efforts to be competitive in 2020—namely, being dramatically outscored on the season and serving as MLB's first COVID-19 outbreak. Nonetheless, the Marlins added Starling Marte to their team, qualified for the funky, phony postseason format, and then made the most of it by defeating a much stronger Cubs squad.

Meanwhile, the Orioles were, as they have been so many times, a cautionary tale. They had stripped down their roster so thoroughly that there was little left to trade, and thus, little to get back. Regardless, they tried to rev up their tank. Like all their other endeavors, they failed at their goal, this time via on-field success. By ripping off a hot streak that had them in the waning days of the season in the one position they emphatically did not want: contention.

⚾   ⚾   ⚾

The wretched con of Major League Baseball in 2020—the one the Orioles are three years into clumsily attempting to exploit—is that its competitive structure is increasingly based on moral hazards. This is not exclusive to Baltimore's station within the league. Slide up the win curve and you can watch the reigning pennant winner trade their homegrown ace two months to the date of him pitching them a few outs away of Game 7. Or, a reigning division champ tossing away the Cy Young runner-up in a salary dump. Like every team selling off their good to great players, they will blame it on an unprecedented revenue dip from the pandemic while refusing to discuss how their decades of record profits factor into their decision making. Team social media accounts boast about cost control they received from trading superstars instead of employing them. "IYKYK" (if you know you know), we were told.

Well, WK.

Luck is the residue of design, sure, but what does it say about a franchise that sees good luck as an impairment instead of a chance to accelerate? And what does it say about a league that not only permits such a design fueled by blind, inflexible subservience to projections, but promotes it?

We're seeing this across the league, but especially in Baltimore, where hubris is veiled as humility, costing Baltimore their best chance at being worth anyone's time for the foreseeable future. When your only rubric is probabilistic thinking performed in service of profitability the only possible end is a self-fulfilling prophecy. There's no going for the gold unless one can get it appraised beforehand. Great game we have here. ◼

—Bradford William Davis is a columnist at the New York Daily News.

Part 2: Player Analysis

PLAYER COMMENTS WITH GRAPHS

Freddy Galvis   SS

Born: 11/14/89   Age: 31   Bats: S   Throws: R
Height: 5'10"   Weight: 195   Origin: International Free Agent, 2006

YEAR	TEAM	LVL	AGE	PA	R	2B	3B	HR	RBI	BB	K	SB	CS	AVG/OBP/SLG
2018	SD	MLB	28	656	62	31	5	13	67	45	147	8	6	.248/.299/.380
2019	TOR	MLB	29	473	55	24	1	18	54	21	112	4	1	.267/.299/.444
2019	CIN	MLB	29	116	12	4	0	5	16	7	33	0	1	.234/.284/.411
2020	CIN	MLB	30	159	18	5	0	7	16	13	30	1	1	.220/.308/.404
2021 FS	BAL	MLB	31	600	64	25	2	20	68	37	133	9	5	.247/.302/.411
2021 DC	BAL	MLB	31	519	56	21	1	17	58	32	115	8	4	.247/.302/.411

Comparables: Greg Gagne, Chris Woodward, Shawon Dunston

Galvis always plays with infectious energy, dreadlocks flying as he pirouettes through the infield dirt to register another improbable assist or bounds from the dugout to congratulate a teammate. His enthusiasm and plus glove in the middle infield will always find him work, but his anemic bat keeps him from being anyone's long-term solution. Galvis continues to launch the occasional home run but rarely walks and doesn't make enough hard contact to make him an asset at the plate. As long as he can flash the leather he's ideally cast as a veteran infield stabilizer who can boost the spirits of a rebuilding club's young pitching staff, which is good work if you can get it.

YEAR	TEAM	LVL	AGE	PA	DRC+	BABIP	BRR	FRAA	WARP
2018	SD	MLB	28	656	81	.304	-1.2	SS(160): -8.9, 2B(5): -0.5	0.4
2019	TOR	MLB	29	473	92	.318	-1.8	SS(103): -2.0, 2B(5): -0.2	1.3
2019	CIN	MLB	29	116	87	.286	-0.6	2B(27): -1.4, SS(7): -0.5	0.0
2020	CIN	MLB	30	159	98	.231	-0.9	SS(33): -0.2, 2B(16): 0.2	0.4
2021 FS	BAL	MLB	31	600	90	.292	0.4	SS -3, 2B 0	0.8
2021 DC	BAL	MLB	31	519	90	.292	0.3	SS -2	0.7

Freddy Galvis, continued

Batted Ball Distribution

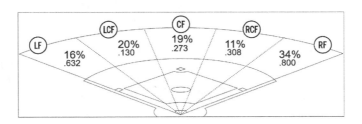

Strike Zone vs LHP   ## Strike Zone vs RHP

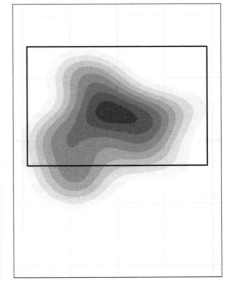

Austin Hays   RF

Born: 07/05/95   Age: 26   Bats: R   Throws: R
Height: 6'0"   Weight: 205   Origin: Round 3, 2016 Draft (#91 overall)

YEAR	TEAM	LVL	AGE	PA	R	2B	3B	HR	RBI	BB	K	SB	CS	AVG/OBP/SLG
2018	ABD	SS	22	39	6	2	0	0	3	2	7	0	0	.189/.231/.243
2018	BOW	AA	22	288	34	12	2	12	43	12	59	6	3	.242/.271/.432
2019	FRE	HI-A	23	40	3	0	0	2	6	1	11	0	0	.162/.200/.324
2019	BOW	AA	23	61	9	5	0	3	11	5	11	3	1	.268/.328/.518
2019	NOR	AAA	23	257	43	16	1	10	27	11	61	6	4	.254/.304/.454
2019	BAL	MLB	23	75	12	6	0	4	13	7	13	2	0	.309/.373/.574
2020	BAL	MLB	24	134	20	2	0	4	9	8	25	2	3	.279/.328/.393
2021 FS	BAL	MLB	25	600	75	26	1	27	70	29	137	5	2	.256/.302/.453
2021 DC	BAL	MLB	25	541	67	23	1	24	63	27	124	4	2	.256/.302/.453

Comparables: Alex Verdugo, Carl Everett, Dale Murphy

If Derek Jeter is Mr. November and Reggie Jackson is Mr. October, Hays is Mr. September. After a hilariously good final month of 2019 that had Orioles fans doing Mike Trout–related play-index searches, Hays came into 2020 with some real hype. And after leading off in center field against Boston on Opening Day, he had a puncher's chance at becoming The Oriole Your Uncle Has Heard Of™. Alas, it was not to be. A slow start and a fractured rib via HBP caused him to miss a month and lose his job in center to Cedric Mullins. But right when the year seemed lost, Hays returned on September 14 and scorched his way to a .377/.404/.585 slash line with great right field defense over the season's final fortnight. Partially because of the injury and partially due to the pandemic-shortened season, we didn't learn anything new about Hays in 2020. He's still only 25 and can really go get it in the outfield, but there's probably not enough power to play in a corner, which means he'll come into 2021 fighting Mullins for the center field job in a crowded outfield.

YEAR	TEAM	LVL	AGE	PA	DRC+	BABIP	BRR	FRAA	WARP
2018	ABD	SS	22	39	92	.233	0.0	RF(5): -0.6	-0.1
2018	BOW	AA	22	288	88	.263	0.9	RF(36): 6.7, LF(16): -0.3, CF(13): -0.1	0.6
2019	FRE	HI-A	23	40	40	.160	0.2	CF(7): -0.7	-0.2
2019	BOW	AA	23	61	142	.286	-1.1	RF(7): 1.2, CF(4): 0.0	0.4
2019	NOR	AAA	23	257	92	.302	4.2	CF(39): 4.8, RF(16): 0.0, LF(1): -0.1	1.3
2019	BAL	MLB	23	75	111	.333	0.8	CF(20): 2.3	0.7
2020	BAL	MLB	24	134	96	.316	-0.2	CF(23): -0.4, LF(10): 0.4, RF(3): -0.6	0.2
2021 FS	BAL	MLB	25	600	100	.296	-0.3	CF 4, LF 0	2.1
2021 DC	BAL	MLB	25	541	100	.296	-0.3	CF 4, LF 0	2.1

Austin Hays, continued

Batted Ball Distribution

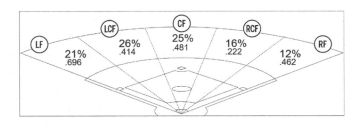

Strike Zone vs LHP   *Strike Zone vs RHP*

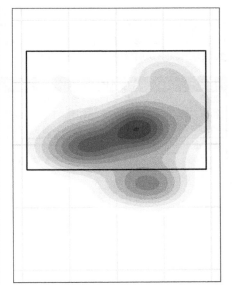

Ryan Mountcastle   1B

Born: 02/18/97   Age: 24   Bats: R   Throws: R
Height: 6'3"   Weight: 210   Origin: Round 1, 2015 Draft (#36 overall)

YEAR	TEAM	LVL	AGE	PA	R	2B	3B	HR	RBI	BB	K	SB	CS	AVG/OBP/SLG
2018	BOW	AA	21	428	63	19	4	13	59	26	79	2	0	.297/.341/.464
2019	NOR	AAA	22	553	81	35	1	25	83	24	130	2	1	.312/.344/.527
2020	BAL	MLB	23	140	12	5	0	5	23	11	30	0	1	.333/.386/.492
2021 FS	BAL	MLB	24	600	70	25	1	25	76	29	150	0	1	.256/.298/.443
2021 DC	BAL	MLB	24	577	67	24	1	24	73	28	145	0	1	.256/.298/.443

Comparables: Dayan Viciedo, Wes Bankston, Brett Wallace

It feels like Mountcastle has been an Orioles prospect since the Ripken days, yet he somehow remains a rookie heading into 2021, despite a 35-game debut campaign. Mountcastle was drafted in the same first round as Alex Bregman and Dansby Swanson, both of whom carry been-around-a-long-while vibes. But after a half-decade in the minors, the Hilltop Fortress finally got his first big-league taste and was superb. You'd bet against him hitting .330 every season, but he's absolutely a Just Knows How To Hit guy who could tickle the .300 mark for the next 10 years. The upside is limited, as he lacks elite exit velocity, swings and misses a tad too much and is underwhelming no matter where he stands in the field. That said, Mountcastle is probably reason no. 1 to actively watch and get excited about the 2021 Orioles.

YEAR	TEAM	LVL	AGE	PA	DRC+	BABIP	BRR	FRAA	WARP
2018	BOW	AA	21	428	117	.339	-1.5	3B(81): -4.9	0.8
2019	NOR	AAA	22	553	114	.370	-0.9	1B(84): -6.1, LF(26): 2.1, 3B(9): -0.1	1.3
2020	BAL	MLB	23	140	104	.398	-0.9	LF(25): -1.7, 1B(10): 0.3	0.0
2021 FS	BAL	MLB	24	600	96	.308	-0.8	1B -1, LF -2	0.4
2021 DC	BAL	MLB	24	577	96	.308	-0.8	1B -1, LF -2	0.4

Ryan Mountcastle, continued

Batted Ball Distribution

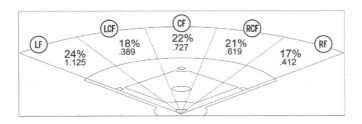

Strike Zone vs LHP   *Strike Zone vs RHP*

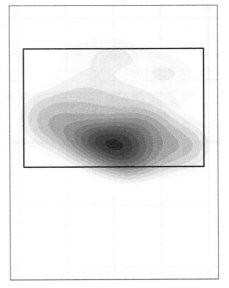

Cedric Mullins CF

Born: 10/01/94   Age: 26   Bats: S   Throws: L
Height: 5'8"   Weight: 175   Origin: Round 13, 2015 Draft (#403 overall)

YEAR	TEAM	LVL	AGE	PA	R	2B	3B	HR	RBI	BB	K	SB	CS	AVG/OBP/SLG
2018	BOW	AA	23	218	36	12	5	6	28	15	28	9	1	.313/.362/.512
2018	NOR	AAA	23	269	41	17	3	6	19	22	39	12	0	.269/.333/.438
2018	BAL	MLB	23	191	23	9	0	4	11	17	37	2	3	.235/.312/.359
2019	BOW	AA	24	226	35	11	0	5	18	22	31	20	3	.271/.341/.402
2019	NOR	AAA	24	306	40	8	2	5	24	25	51	13	4	.205/.272/.306
2019	BAL	MLB	24	74	7	0	2	0	4	4	14	1	0	.094/.181/.156
2020	BAL	MLB	25	153	16	4	3	3	12	8	37	7	2	.271/.315/.407
2021 FS	BAL	MLB	26	600	67	21	2	17	53	41	140	14	4	.217/.278/.359
2021 DC	BAL	MLB	26	295	33	10	1	8	26	20	69	7	2	.217/.278/.359

Comparables: Sil Campusano, Milt Cuyler, Cory Sullivan

After a putrid 2019 season in the bigs and bouncing around various Orioles eastern seaboard affiliates, Mullins was a bit of an afterthought heading into 2020. Then, an Austin Hays injury led to a lot of Mullins playing time, and he took advantage. The first thing to know is that he's stupendous in center. Questions about his bat remain. If he can keep his OPS in the .700-plus range and perform on the basepaths, he's César Hernández but with top-tier defense in center. That's a pretty good player. But it's important to keep in mind that the difference between that and Billy Hamilton is a slippery slope.

YEAR	TEAM	LVL	AGE	PA	DRC+	BABIP	BRR	FRAA	WARP
2018	BOW	AA	23	218	134	.339	2.4	CF(43): 0.4, LF(2): 0.5	1.5
2018	NOR	AAA	23	269	117	.298	2.2	CF(60): 0.2	1.3
2018	BAL	MLB	23	191	82	.279	-0.6	CF(45): -3.8, LF(1): -0.0	-0.2
2019	BOW	AA	24	226	127	.293	2.8	CF(31): 0.9, LF(19): 0.1	1.7
2019	NOR	AAA	24	306	50	.231	1.8	CF(56): 4.1, LF(6): -0.6	-0.3
2019	BAL	MLB	24	74	56	.118	0.5	CF(22): 1.4	0.0
2020	BAL	MLB	25	153	67	.350	0.5	CF(41): 5.1, LF(4): -0.1, RF(4): -0.5	0.4
2021 FS	BAL	MLB	26	600	72	.260	1.1	CF 1, LF 0	-0.2
2021 DC	BAL	MLB	26	295	72	.260	0.5	CF 1, LF 0	-0.2

Cedric Mullins, continued

Batted Ball Distribution

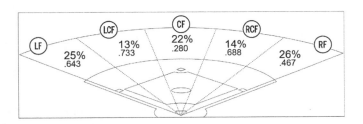

Strike Zone vs LHP   ### Strike Zone vs RHP

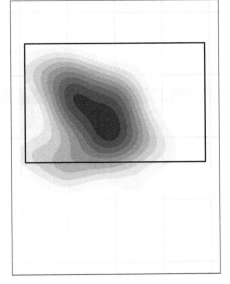

Rio Ruiz 3B

Born: 05/22/94   Age: 27   Bats: L   Throws: R
Height: 6'1"   Weight: 215   Origin: Round 4, 2012 Draft (#129 overall)

YEAR	TEAM	LVL	AGE	PA	R	2B	3B	HR	RBI	BB	K	SB	CS	AVG/OBP/SLG
2018	GWN	AAA	24	541	72	25	4	9	72	40	90	2	1	.269/.322/.390
2018	ATL	MLB	24	15	1	0	0	0	0	2	5	0	0	.083/.267/.083
2019	BAL	MLB	25	413	35	13	2	12	46	40	88	0	1	.232/.306/.376
2020	BAL	MLB	26	204	25	11	0	9	32	17	46	1	2	.222/.286/.427
2021 FS	BAL	MLB	27	600	66	24	2	19	65	59	145	0	1	.230/.309/.395
2021 DC	BAL	MLB	27	520	57	21	2	17	56	51	126	0	1	.230/.309/.395

Comparables: Phil Nevin, Greg Norton, Russ Davis

Ok, blind test. Would you rather have Player A or B? Player A: 2.2 WARP, 16 HR, 140 DRC+, .304/.370/.580. Player B: 0.2 WARP, 9 HR, 96 DRC+, .222/.310/398. Same position, but the defensive numbers like Player A a tick more. Who'd you take? Player A? It's not even close? Well, fine then... Player A is Manny Machado and Player B is Ruiz. Knowing what you know now, would you still take Player A? You would. Ok. Well, that's unfortunate because Player A is not on the Orioles anymore. He's on the Padres now doing cool stuff. Ruiz is on the Orioles, though! He's not Manny Machado—as was just proven—but he's fine. The Orioles don't have any third basemen in the minors knocking on the door, so Ruiz probably gets another year as a transitional filler. He's not horrible at anything or spectacular at anything, and he's definitely not Manny Machado.

YEAR	TEAM	LVL	AGE	PA	DRC+	BABIP	BRR	FRAA	WARP
2018	GWN	AAA	24	541	95	.311	1.8	3B(49): 2.3, 1B(35): 1.5, LF(20): 0.1	0.4
2018	ATL	MLB	24	15	77	.143	-0.1	3B(1): -0.2	0.0
2019	BAL	MLB	25	413	81	.272	-1.4	3B(114): 2.3, 1B(12): 0.3, 2B(1): 0.0	0.6
2020	BAL	MLB	26	204	96	.244	0.2	3B(53): -1.2, 2B(1): 0.0, LF(1): -0.0	0.2
2021 FS	BAL	MLB	27	600	90	.280	-0.7	3B 0, 1B 0	0.3
2021 DC	BAL	MLB	27	520	90	.280	-0.6	3B 0	0.3

Rio Ruiz, continued

Batted Ball Distribution

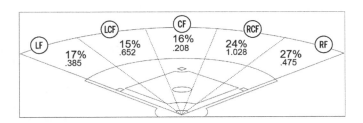

Strike Zone vs LHP

Strike Zone vs RHP

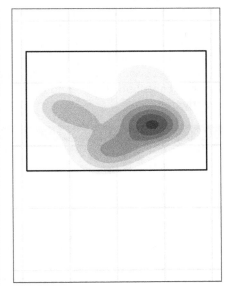

Baltimore Orioles 2021

Anthony Santander   LF

Born: 10/19/94   Age: 26   Bats: S   Throws: R
Height: 6'2"   Weight: 225   Origin: International Free Agent, 2011

YEAR	TEAM	LVL	AGE	PA	R	2B	3B	HR	RBI	BB	K	SB	CS	AVG/OBP/SLG
2018	ABD	SS	23	31	6	5	0	1	5	2	5	2	0	.286/.355/.571
2018	BOW	AA	23	222	26	9	3	5	22	10	32	4	1	.258/.293/.402
2018	NOR	AAA	23	47	3	3	0	2	7	2	9	0	0	.182/.213/.386
2018	BAL	MLB	23	108	8	5	1	1	6	6	21	1	0	.198/.250/.297
2019	NOR	AAA	24	209	30	15	0	5	28	13	38	3	2	.259/.311/.415
2019	BAL	MLB	24	405	46	20	1	20	59	19	86	1	2	.261/.297/.476
2020	BAL	MLB	25	165	24	13	1	11	32	10	25	0	1	.261/.315/.575
2021 FS	BAL	MLB	26	600	78	30	1	28	74	34	125	1	1	.252/.305/.464
2021 DC	BAL	MLB	26	597	77	30	1	28	74	34	124	1	1	.252/.305/.464

Comparables: Butch Huskey, Jeff Francoeur, Shawn Green

Before an oblique injury ended his season on September 4, Santander was like a ninth-grader before they go on Acutane: the breakout story of the year. Acne jokes aside, "The Bank" was a revelation for the O's, cashing out 11 homers while playing above-average defense in right. Even though he debuted back in 2017, the pride of Margarita Island, Venezuela is only entering his age-26 season. That's sneaky young. Younger than Jake Cronenworth, Shohei Ohtani and Clint Frazier, all of whom had fewer home runs than Santander in 2020. For bad teams to get good, you need a couple waiver claims to break right and develop into real contributors. The smooth-swinging Santander is starting to look like exactly that.

YEAR	TEAM	LVL	AGE	PA	DRC+	BABIP	BRR	FRAA	WARP
2018	ABD	SS	23	31	130	.318	0.2	RF(5): -0.2	0.0
2018	BOW	AA	23	222	87	.282	0.7	RF(35): -3.6, LF(14): -1.4	-0.7
2018	NOR	AAA	23	47	79	.176	-0.1	RF(8): 1.1, LF(2): -0.3	0.0
2018	BAL	MLB	23	108	74	.241	0.0	RF(29): 0.8, LF(1): -0.0	0.0
2019	NOR	AAA	24	209	84	.298	1.1	RF(35): 1.8, LF(8): -0.9	0.2
2019	BAL	MLB	24	405	97	.285	-0.5	RF(50): -4.8, LF(40): 8.3, CF(24): 3.8	1.6
2020	BAL	MLB	25	165	138	.248	0.7	RF(35): 0.5, LF(2): 0.0	1.4
2021 FS	BAL	MLB	26	600	102	.280	-0.9	RF 3, LF 0	1.7
2021 DC	BAL	MLB	26	597	102	.280	-0.9	RF 3	1.6

Anthony Santander, continued

Batted Ball Distribution

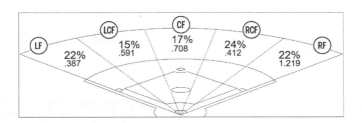

Strike Zone vs LHP   Strike Zone vs RHP

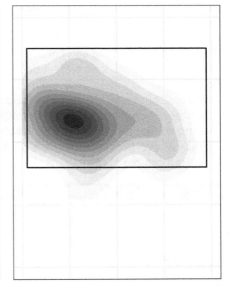

Pedro Severino   C

Born: 07/20/93   Age: 27   Bats: R   Throws: R
Height: 6'1"   Weight: 220   Origin: International Free Agent, 2010

YEAR	TEAM	LVL	AGE	PA	R	2B	3B	HR	RBI	BB	K	SB	CS	AVG/OBP/SLG
2018	SYR	AAA	24	136	14	5	1	6	13	5	23	0	0	.269/.294/.462
2018	WAS	MLB	24	213	14	9	0	2	15	18	47	1	0	.168/.254/.247
2019	BAL	MLB	25	341	37	13	0	13	44	29	73	3	1	.249/.321/.420
2020	BAL	MLB	26	178	17	5	1	5	21	16	40	1	0	.250/.322/.388
2021 FS	BAL	MLB	27	600	65	24	1	20	68	44	138	2	1	.241/.305/.399
2021 DC	BAL	MLB	27	298	32	12	0	10	34	22	68	0	1	.241/.305/.399

Comparables: Sal Fasano, Bruce Maxwell, Chris Snyder

Severino is the most fun second-division starter, first-division backup catcher in baseball. He gestures constantly, and he loves a good point at his pitcher after a well-located heater. No one slaps the dirt harder to emphasize that he wants a curveball down, and if someone hits a bomb, you can count on a heavy head drop or

YEAR	TEAM	P. COUNT	FRM RUNS	BLK RUNS	THRW RUNS	TOT RUNS
2018	WAS	8442	0.3	0.2	0.1	0.6
2018	SYR	4330	1.4	0.0	0.0	1.4
2019	BAL	12991	-9.6	-4.1	-0.2	-13.9
2020	BAL	4698	-3.2	-0.8	-0.1	-4.0
2021	BAL	9620	-0.5	-1.1	0.6	-1.0
2021	BAL	9620	-0.5	-2.6	0.6	-2.5

a fierce ripping off of the catcher's mask. Severino is super lovable, incredibly fun to watch and will be a perfect backup to Adley Rutschman whenever the chosen son arrives in Baltimore. There was a moment in 2020 after Severino got off to a really hot start where some folks were like "hmmmmmmm, maybe there's more here," but a slow September doused any hope of a real breakout. Severino is what he is now: a dependable, well-liked presence behind the plate, a slightly above-average hitter for a backstop in the modern game and the best Dominican catcher in the AL East (sorry Gary Sánchez).

YEAR	TEAM	LVL	AGE	PA	DRC+	BABIP	BRR	FRAA	WARP
2018	SYR	AAA	24	136	93	.284	-2.1	C(32): 1.1	0.3
2018	WAS	MLB	24	213	60	.211	-0.1	C(67): -0.0	0.0
2019	BAL	MLB	25	341	90	.285	-2.4	C(89): -13.8	-0.3
2020	BAL	MLB	26	178	97	.304	-0.5	C(35): -0.4	0.0
2021 FS	BAL	MLB	27	600	89	.288	-0.8	C -2	1.3
2021 DC	BAL	MLB	27	298	89	.288	-0.4	C -1	0.6

Pedro Severino, continued

Batted Ball Distribution

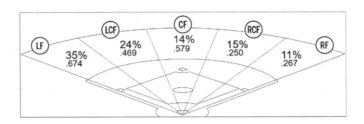

Strike Zone vs LHP

Strike Zone vs RHP

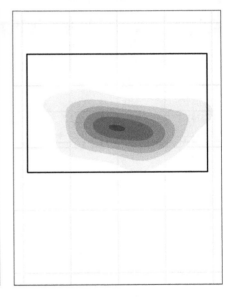

Pat Valaika   3B

Born: 09/09/92   Age: 28   Bats: R   Throws: R
Height: 5'11"   Weight: 210   Origin: Round 9, 2013 Draft (#259 overall)

YEAR	TEAM	LVL	AGE	PA	R	2B	3B	HR	RBI	BB	K	SB	CS	AVG/OBP/SLG
2018	ABQ	AAA	25	147	13	4	1	8	20	7	30	1	1	.216/.252/.432
2018	COL	MLB	25	133	8	5	0	2	5	9	30	0	0	.156/.214/.246
2019	ABQ	AAA	26	383	60	26	1	22	75	27	90	5	1	.320/.364/.589
2019	COL	MLB	26	86	11	5	1	1	4	7	34	0	0	.190/.256/.316
2020	BAL	MLB	27	150	24	4	0	8	16	8	34	0	2	.277/.315/.475
2021 FS	BAL	MLB	28	600	66	24	1	28	74	33	166	2	2	.232/.279/.427
2021 DC	BAL	MLB	28	186	20	7	0	8	22	10	51	0	1	.232/.279/.427

Comparables: Orlando Miller, Javier Báez, Jonathan Villar

Is Valaika the second coming of DJ LeMahieu? Not hardly, but he *is* another Colorado infielder who left Coors Field only to immediately post significantly better offensive stats. Valaika's playing in 52-of-60 games is a sure sign that some things went wrong in Baltimore, but if he keeps it up with the stick, he'll remain a solid utility option.

YEAR	TEAM	LVL	AGE	PA	DRC+	BABIP	BRR	FRAA	WARP
2018	ABQ	AAA	25	147	63	.216	-0.6	2B(9): 0.1, SS(9): 0.4, 1B(8): -0.3	-0.3
2018	COL	MLB	25	133	62	.189	0.3	2B(17): -0.6, 1B(15): -0.4, 3B(8): 0.0	-0.3
2019	ABQ	AAA	26	383	118	.370	1.0	2B(36): 1.1, 3B(18): 1.6, SS(18): -1.4	2.3
2019	COL	MLB	26	86	60	.318	0.0	2B(13): -0.8, SS(7): 0.1, 3B(3): 0.1	-0.2
2020	BAL	MLB	27	150	110	.313	0.6	SS(24): 0.0, 1B(13): -0.4, 2B(13): 1.2	0.7
2021 FS	BAL	MLB	28	600	83	.280	-0.7	2B 0, 3B 1	0.6
2021 DC	BAL	MLB	28	186	83	.280	-0.2	2B 0, 3B 0	0.2

Pat Valaika, continued

Batted Ball Distribution

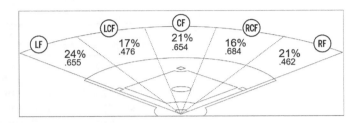

Strike Zone vs LHP   *Strike Zone vs RHP*

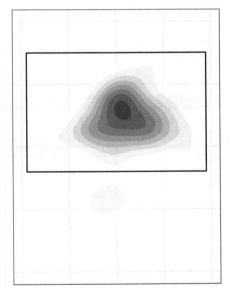

Keegan Akin LHP

Born: 04/01/95   Age: 26   Bats: L   Throws: L
Height: 6'0"   Weight: 225   Origin: Round 2, 2016 Draft (#54 overall)

YEAR	TEAM	LVL	AGE	W	L	SV	G	GS	IP	H	HR	BB/9	K/9	K	GB%	BABIP
2018	BOW	AA	23	14	7	0	25	25	137²	114	16	3.8	9.3	142	31.7%	.278
2019	NOR	AAA	24	6	7	0	25	24	112¹	109	10	4.9	10.5	131	32.4%	.333
2020	BAL	MLB	25	1	2	0	8	6	25²	27	3	3.5	12.3	35	34.3%	.358
2021 FS	BAL	MLB	26	9	9	0	26	26	150	141	28	4.4	10.1	167	33.0%	.296
2021 DC	BAL	MLB	26	7	7	0	25	25	114	107	21	4.4	10.1	127	33.0%	.296

Comparables: Conner Menez, Taylor Hearn, Anthony Misiewicz

That a 6-footer with a 92 mph fastball led all Orioles pitchers in strikeouts per nine in 2020 probably says more about the Orioles staff than it does about Akin. While he's certainly not the second coming of Nolan Ryan, the lefty flashed an interesting arsenal in his big-league debut. Built like a clenched fist, Akin uses a high-spin fastball to get more swings up and above the zone than you'd predict from the velocity. For that shtick to work long-term, he must have command of the off-speed stuff arm-side, which he did when he was at his best (a scoreless nine-strikeout performance against Atlanta in September). Think Mark Buehrle with worse command and better stuff—basically a stout lefty who works quickly and relies on nibbling the edges of the zone. He's almost certainly not a frontline guy, but a rotation workhorse who can sponge up innings and get you through the order twice without getting his teeth kicked in? That'll play.

YEAR	TEAM	LVL	AGE	WHIP	ERA	DRA-	WARP	MPH	FB%	WHF	CSP
2018	BOW	AA	23	1.25	3.27	87	2.0				
2019	NOR	AAA	24	1.51	4.73	89	2.6				
2020	BAL	MLB	25	1.44	4.56	85	0.4	94.2	62.0%	28.5%	
2021 FS	BAL	MLB	26	1.43	4.90	105	1.0	94.2	62.0%	28.5%	52.0%
2021 DC	BAL	MLB	26	1.43	4.90	105	0.7	94.2	62.0%	28.5%	52.0%

Keegan Akin, continued

Pitch Shape vs LHH

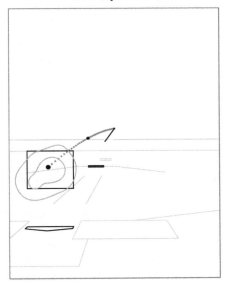

Pitch Shape vs RHH

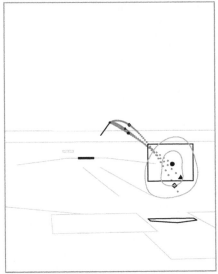

Type	Frequency	Velocity	H Movement	V Movement
● Fastball	62.0%	92 [98]	9.9 [85]	-13.2 [106]
▲ Changeup	17.4%	81.3 [85]	14.1 [87]	-29.9 [93]
▽ Slider	10.8%	80.6 [85]	-5.4 [101]	-40 [82]
◇ Curveball	9.8%	77.1 [94]	-7.8 [101]	-50 [96]

Shawn Armstrong   RHP

Born: 09/11/90   Age: 30   Bats: R   Throws: R
Height: 6'2"   Weight: 225   Origin: Round 18, 2011 Draft (#548 overall)

YEAR	TEAM	LVL	AGE	W	L	SV	G	GS	IP	H	HR	BB/9	K/9	K	GB%	BABIP
2018	TAC	AAA	27	2	5	15	49	0	56	38	3	4.2	13.2	82	32.8%	.302
2018	SEA	MLB	27	0	1	1	14	0	14²	9	1	1.8	9.2	15	41.7%	.229
2019	BAL	MLB	28	1	0	4	51	0	54¹	58	7	4.3	9.9	60	30.2%	.336
2019	SEA	MLB	28	0	1	0	4	0	3²	8	1	7.4	7.4	3	18.8%	.500
2020	BAL	MLB	29	2	0	0	14	0	15	9	1	1.8	8.4	14	43.6%	.211
2021 FS	BAL	MLB	30	2	2	6	57	0	50	42	7	3.9	9.9	54	36.1%	.277
2021 DC	BAL	MLB	30	3	3	6	64	0	71.3	60	10	3.9	9.9	78	36.1%	.277

Comparables: Nick Wittgren, Santiago Casilla, Tommy Kahnle

In the age of advanced metrics, it's easy to get lost in the numbers and lose focus on what they ultimately mean. Armstrong has a high-spin cutter. It has more spin than Kenley Jansen's cutter, which might be impressive if Casey Sadler (who spent 2019 on the Rays and Dodgers—wrong year, Casey—but 2020 on the Cubs and Mariners) didn't have a *higher* spin cutter than Armstrong. Sadler had a 5.12 ERA. Armstrong's strikeout per inning and ERA around 2.00 are promising indicators. Of course, Sadler checked both of those boxes in 2019 before regression hit hard the following year, and Armstrong's hit suppression doesn't look to be any more sustainable. He limits the free passes, though, and as far as waiver pickups go, he looks to be a quality one for Baltimore. The role of fifth most famous American Armstrong is wide open behind Neil, Louis, and Billie Joe. We see no reason Shawn can't claim the spot.

YEAR	TEAM	LVL	AGE	WHIP	ERA	DRA-	WARP	MPH	FB%	WHF	CSP
2018	TAC	AAA	27	1.14	1.77	46	1.9				
2018	SEA	MLB	27	0.82	1.23	98	0.1	95.0	78.4%	24.3%	
2019	BAL	MLB	28	1.55	5.13	111	0.0	94.9	88.2%	26.3%	
2019	SEA	MLB	28	3.00	14.73	154	-0.1	93.9	78.9%	31.2%	
2020	BAL	MLB	29	0.80	1.80	89	0.2	95.3	89.0%	26.2%	
2021 FS	BAL	MLB	30	1.27	3.88	87	0.6	95.0	87.2%	26.5%	50.2%
2021 DC	BAL	MLB	30	1.27	3.88	87	0.9	95.0	87.2%	26.5%	50.2%

Shawn Armstrong, continued

Pitch Shape vs LHH

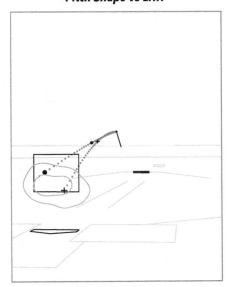

Pitch Shape vs RHH

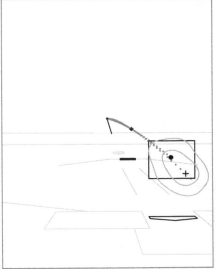

Type	Frequency	Velocity	H Movement	V Movement
● Fastball	43.0%	93.8 [104]	-4.1 [113]	-12.2 [108]
+ Cutter	46.0%	88.7 [103]	6.2 [128]	-27.4 [87]
◇ Curveball	11.0%	82.1 [114]	11.2 [115]	-41.5 [115]

Thomas Eshelman   RHP

Born: 06/20/94   Age: 27   Bats: R   Throws: R
Height: 6'3"   Weight: 210   Origin: Round 2, 2015 Draft (#46 overall)

YEAR	TEAM	LVL	AGE	W	L	SV	G	GS	IP	H	HR	BB/9	K/9	K	GB%	BABIP
2018	LHV	AAA	24	2	13	0	27	26	140¹	189	21	2.9	6.7	104	40.6%	.358
2019	REA	AA	25	0	3	0	6	6	28²	43	4	1.9	8.2	26	41.6%	.406
2019	LHV	AAA	25	1	1	0	4	4	26	23	3	1.7	8.0	23	48.6%	.282
2019	NOR	AAA	25	2	1	0	7	6	38¹	43	6	1.6	6.6	28	40.8%	.301
2019	BAL	MLB	25	1	2	0	10	4	36	47	12	2.8	5.5	22	33.1%	.297
2020	BAL	MLB	26	3	1	0	12	4	34²	34	7	2.3	4.2	16	35.9%	.245
2021 FS	BAL	MLB	27	2	3	0	57	0	50	55	11	2.4	6.1	34	37.5%	.283

Comparables: Walker Lockett, Drew Anderson, Mike Wright

There's something exhilarating about watching Eshelman pitch. The endorphin rush from jumping out of a plane or bungee jumping off a cliff? It's like that, but with loopy curveballs. Only the ever-present proximity to complete and total disaster can truly make you feel alive. Eshelman is Man on Wire, a pitcher living on the edge and occasionally beyond it. His is a kitchen-sink approach. He boasts five distinct pitches, none of which he threw more than 24 percent of the time, all of which are predisposed to be disposed over a fence by a Yankee. A true corner-nibbler with the fourth-lowest average fastball velocity of any starter, Eshelman survived his way to a 3.89 ERA in 2020 by sequencing backward, by hitting his spots, by crossing his fingers. To watch him pitch is to watch him stumble into the darkness, like a blindfolded toddler running toward a hive of wasps; to hold your breath and pray as Luke Voit pops an 85 mph fastball up to second base. Then, like the parent of that toddler, you exhale and await whatever comes next.

YEAR	TEAM	LVL	AGE	WHIP	ERA	DRA-	WARP	MPH	FB%	WHF	CSP
2018	LHV	AAA	24	1.67	5.84	101	0.9				
2019	REA	AA	25	1.71	6.28	144	-0.7				
2019	LHV	AAA	25	1.08	2.77	103	0.4				
2019	NOR	AAA	25	1.30	4.70	92	0.8				
2019	BAL	MLB	25	1.61	6.50	179	-1.2	87.6	45.8%	15.4%	
2020	BAL	MLB	26	1.24	3.89	145	-0.5	88.1	43.8%	17.3%	
2021 FS	BAL	MLB	27	1.37	5.33	117	-0.2	87.9	44.6%	16.5%	51.6%

Thomas Eshelman, continued

Pitch Shape vs LHH

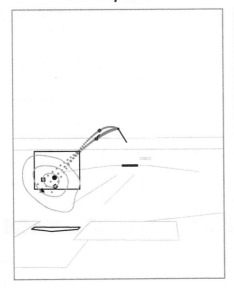

Pitch Shape vs RHH

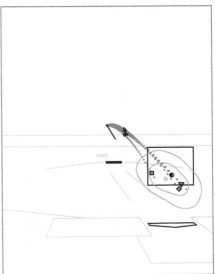

Type	Frequency	Velocity	H Movement	V Movement
● Fastball	23.4%	86.1 [79]	-0.7 [129]	-21.7 [82]
□ Sinker	19.8%	86.7 [71]	-9 [130]	-20.9 [99]
▲ Changeup	12.7%	79.5 [78]	-5.2 [134]	-31 [90]
▽ Slider	20.4%	78.1 [74]	8.4 [112]	-36.7 [91]
◇ Curveball	22.4%	76.8 [93]	5.5 [92]	-46.3 [105]

Paul Fry   LHP

Born: 07/26/92   Age: 28   Bats: L   Throws: L
Height: 6'0"   Weight: 205   Origin: Round 17, 2013 Draft (#507 overall)

YEAR	TEAM	LVL	AGE	W	L	SV	G	GS	IP	H	HR	BB/9	K/9	K	GB%	BABIP
2018	BOW	AA	25	3	0	2	15	0	19	10	2	5.2	13.3	28	64.9%	.229
2018	NOR	AAA	25	0	1	0	13	1	23¹	22	2	1.5	11.2	29	51.7%	.351
2018	BAL	MLB	25	1	2	2	35	0	37²	33	1	3.6	8.6	36	57.7%	.311
2019	BAL	MLB	26	1	9	3	66	0	57¹	54	7	4.6	8.6	55	57.0%	.299
2020	BAL	MLB	27	1	0	0	22	0	22	22	3	3.7	11.9	29	57.6%	.339
2021 FS	BAL	MLB	28	2	2	0	57	0	50	44	5	4.4	10.3	57	53.6%	.305
2021 DC	BAL	MLB	28	3	3	0	64	0	71.3	63	7	4.4	10.3	82	53.6%	.305

Comparables: J.B. Wendelken, Dovydas Neverauskas, Dan Altavilla

With two new ticks on his fastball, Fry took a nice jump forward with a basic but effective fastball-slider combo that gave lefties a tough time. Having the best year of one's life occur in 2020 is a dubious honor, but one Fry can reasonably claim. Every bullpen needs the Second-Best Lefty Reliever™, and he is definitely that. All that to say: he's not a big deal, but more of a Paul Fry.

YEAR	TEAM	LVL	AGE	WHIP	ERA	DRA-	WARP	MPH	FB%	WHF	CSP
2018	BOW	AA	25	1.11	2.84	56	0.5				
2018	NOR	AAA	25	1.11	3.47	51	0.7				
2018	BAL	MLB	25	1.27	3.35	93	0.3	93.2	56.4%	25.4%	
2019	BAL	MLB	26	1.45	5.34	97	0.4	92.5	52.4%	25.9%	
2020	BAL	MLB	27	1.41	2.45	65	0.6	94.1	53.5%	29.2%	
2021 FS	BAL	MLB	28	1.38	4.13	91	0.5	93.1	53.3%	26.8%	46.6%
2021 DC	BAL	MLB	28	1.38	4.13	91	0.7	93.1	53.3%	26.8%	46.6%

Paul Fry, continued

Pitch Shape vs LHH

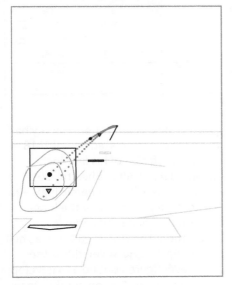

Pitch Shape vs RHH

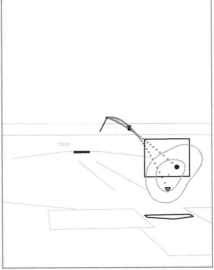

Type	Frequency	Velocity	H Movement	V Movement
● Fastball	53.5%	92.9 [101]	5.1 [108]	-16.2 [97]
▽ Slider	45.7%	84.9 [104]	-13.5 [131]	-38.9 [85]

Hunter Harvey   RHP

Born: 12/09/94   Age: 26   Bats: R   Throws: R
Height: 6'3"   Weight: 210   Origin: Round 1, 2013 Draft (#22 overall)

YEAR	TEAM	LVL	AGE	W	L	SV	G	GS	IP	H	HR	BB/9	K/9	K	GB%	BABIP
2018	BOW	AA	23	1	2	0	9	9	32^1	36	3	2.5	8.4	30	35.1%	.351
2019	BOW	AA	24	2	5	1	14	11	59	63	14	3.2	9.3	61	37.9%	.316
2019	NOR	AAA	24	1	1	0	12	0	16^2	13	2	2.7	11.9	22	38.1%	.282
2019	BAL	MLB	24	1	0	0	7	0	6^1	3	1	5.7	15.6	11	54.5%	.200
2020	BAL	MLB	25	0	2	0	10	0	8^2	8	2	2.1	6.2	6	39.3%	.231
2021 FS	BAL	MLB	26	2	2	19	57	0	50	47	8	3.7	9.0	50	38.4%	.289
2021 DC	BAL	MLB	26	3	3	19	64	0	71.3	67	12	3.7	9.0	71	38.4%	.289

Comparables: Keury Mella, Jake McGee, Chase De Jong

Pitchers and their injuries. Since joining the Orioles' organization, Harvey has broken his tibula, had Tommy John surgery on his elbow, missed half of 2018 to shoulder soreness and even lost all the skin on the left side of his face in a gasoline accident. Whoops, sorry, sorry … wrong Harvey. After a healthy 2019 that included a brief big-league stint where he showed off his dynamic high-90s heater and devastating curve, 2020 was back to the injury woes for the long-haired right-hander. A forearm strain kept him on the shelf until early September, and he never got going after he returned. The stuff is still sexy as hell and the ceiling remains a high-leverage, late-inning guy. However, this is the exact type of arm that, in the past, the Orioles never figured out how to develop correctly or keep healthy enough, then ended up as an All-Star on another team (see: Arrieta, Jake). Hopefully, Harvey can stay on the mound in 2021 and fulfill his destiny as Baltimore's flame-throwing closer of the future.

YEAR	TEAM	LVL	AGE	WHIP	ERA	DRA-	WARP	MPH	FB%	WHF	CSP
2018	BOW	AA	23	1.39	5.57	89	0.4				
2019	BOW	AA	24	1.42	5.19	132	-1.1				
2019	NOR	AAA	24	1.08	4.32	61	0.5				
2019	BAL	MLB	24	1.11	1.42	75	0.1	99.5	69.6%	25.4%	
2020	BAL	MLB	25	1.15	4.15	113	0.0	98.9	77.2%	23.3%	
2021 FS	BAL	MLB	26	1.35	4.60	101	0.2	99.1	74.3%	24.1%	49.0%
2021 DC	BAL	MLB	26	1.35	4.60	101	0.3	99.1	74.3%	24.1%	49.0%

Hunter Harvey, continued

Pitch Shape vs LHH

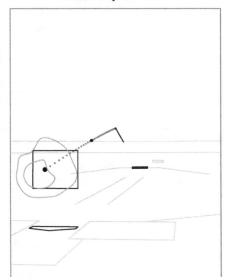

Pitch Shape vs RHH

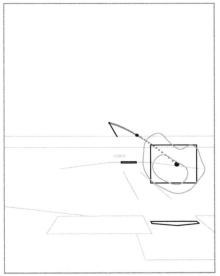

Type	Frequency	Velocity	H Movement	V Movement
● Fastball	77.2%	97.3 [115]	-7.7 [95]	-10.4 [113]
▲ Changeup	8.3%	90.5 [121]	-11.6 [101]	-24.6 [108]
◇ Curveball	14.5%	83.2 [118]	4.9 [89]	-43.6 [111]

Dean Kremer   RHP

Born: 01/07/96   Age: 25   Bats: R   Throws: R
Height: 6'3"   Weight: 185   Origin: Round 14, 2016 Draft (#431 overall)

YEAR	TEAM	LVL	AGE	W	L	SV	G	GS	IP	H	HR	BB/9	K/9	K	GB%	BABIP
2018	RC	HI-A	22	5	3	0	16	16	79	67	7	3.0	13.0	114	39.9%	.353
2018	BOW	AA	22	4	2	0	8	8	45^1	38	3	3.4	10.5	53	37.9%	.315
2018	TUL	AA	22	1	0	0	1	1	7	3	0	3.9	14.1	11	75.0%	.250
2019	FRE	HI-A	23	0	0	0	2	2	9^2	6	0	3.7	13.0	14	20.0%	.300
2019	BOW	AA	23	9	4	0	15	15	84^2	75	9	3.1	9.2	87	41.1%	.299
2019	NOR	AAA	23	0	2	0	4	4	19^1	30	2	1.9	9.8	21	36.5%	.467
2020	BAL	MLB	24	1	1	0	4	4	18^2	15	0	5.8	10.6	22	30.6%	.306
2021 FS	*BAL*	*MLB*	*25*	*9*	*8*	*0*	*26*	*26*	*150*	*135*	*27*	*3.2*	*9.4*	*156*	*37.0%*	*.280*
2021 DC	*BAL*	*MLB*	*25*	*7*	*7*	*0*	*25*	*25*	*116.3*	*105*	*21*	*3.2*	*9.4*	*121*	*37.0%*	*.280*

Comparables: T.J. Zeuch, Ryan Helsley, Robert Dugger

When he debuted on September 6 (25th anniversary of Ripken's 2,131), Kremer became the first Israeli to pitch in the big leagues. His four-start debut showed glimpses of why he was a key part of the Manny Machado deal. He did enough with his fastball-curve-cutter combo over his first three starts to overcome a lot of hard contact before the gravitational forces of baseball caught up to him in a disastrous final outing against Boston. The curveball is long and loopy; it has good shape but lacks real bite and operates in a slower-than-average 75 mph range. It's not a nasty, gif-able breaking ball, but he commands it and hides it well enough that it's still an effective offering. Kremer should spend most of 2021 in Baltimore's rotation, and while every indicator points towards a reliable back-end starter, he'll get every opportunity to prove he's more dynamic than that.

YEAR	TEAM	LVL	AGE	WHIP	ERA	DRA-	WARP	MPH	FB%	WHF	CSP
2018	RC	HI-A	22	1.18	3.30	67	1.8				
2018	BOW	AA	22	1.21	2.58	76	0.9				
2018	TUL	AA	22	0.86	0.00	37	0.3				
2019	FRE	HI-A	23	1.03	0.00	73	0.2				
2019	BOW	AA	23	1.23	2.98	96	0.3				
2019	NOR	AAA	23	1.76	8.84	156	-0.2				
2020	BAL	MLB	24	1.45	4.82	96	0.2	95.2	51.2%	26.4%	
2021 FS	*BAL*	*MLB*	*25*	*1.26*	*4.11*	*92*	*2.1*	*95.2*	*51.2%*	*26.4%*	*50.8%*
2021 DC	*BAL*	*MLB*	*25*	*1.26*	*4.11*	*92*	*1.6*	*95.2*	*51.2%*	*26.4%*	*50.8%*

Dean Kremer, continued

Pitch Shape vs LHH

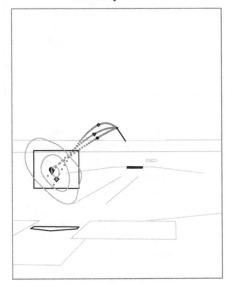

Pitch Shape vs RHH

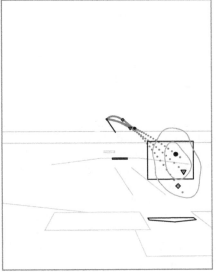

Type	Frequency	Velocity	H Movement	V Movement
● Fastball	51.2%	93.1 [101]	-8.9 [89]	-12.6 [107]
▽ Slider	19.1%	87.1 [114]	3.9 [95]	-26 [123]
◇ Curveball	27.2%	75.6 [88]	8.3 [103]	-58 [79]

Baltimore Orioles 2021

Travis Lakins Sr.   RHP

Born: 06/29/94   Age: 27   Bats: R   Throws: R
Height: 6'1"   Weight: 215   Origin: Round 6, 2015 Draft (#171 overall)

YEAR	TEAM	LVL	AGE	W	L	SV	G	GS	IP	H	HR	BB/9	K/9	K	GB%	BABIP
2018	POR	AA	24	2	2	1	26	6	38	27	3	3.1	9.9	42	47.5%	.250
2018	WOR	AAA	24	1	0	2	10	0	16¹	11	0	2.8	8.3	15	44.4%	.244
2019	WOR	AAA	25	3	4	6	40	1	45	46	4	4.6	8.4	42	39.6%	.328
2019	BOS	MLB	25	0	1	0	16	3	23¹	23	1	3.9	6.9	18	46.6%	.306
2020	BAL	MLB	26	3	2	1	22	0	25²	25	2	4.6	8.8	25	38.2%	.311
2021 FS	BAL	MLB	27	2	3	0	57	0	50	48	8	4.6	8.4	46	41.1%	.291
2021 DC	BAL	MLB	27	3	3	0	64	0	57	55	9	4.6	8.4	53	41.1%	.291

Comparables: Trevor Gott, Victor Alcántara, Michael Lorenzen

The three main characters of the 2019 Orioles bullpen—Miguel Castro, Richard Bleier and Mychal Givens—were all dealt away from Baltimore during the season. The shuffled bullpen chairs of a club that won just shy of 42 percent of its games understandably don't make national headlines, but those empty spots had to go somewhere. That somewhere was Lakins. With Lakins, the Orioles' bullpen strategy of scooping dudes off the waiver wire and seeing what happens worked pretty well. He led the team in innings out of the bullpen to the tune of a sub-three ERA. Now, the advanced metrics aren't too kind—looking at you, 4.89 DRA—but the stuff is playable at the big-league level. Lakins' repertoire includes a high-spin curveball with a hard cutter and a league-average fastball. It's nothing sexy, and he doesn't have the ceiling to throw in high-leverage spots for a good team, but a valuable middle-relief innings sponge seems like an attainable role.

YEAR	TEAM	LVL	AGE	WHIP	ERA	DRA-	WARP	MPH	FB%	WHF	CSP
2018	POR	AA	24	1.05	2.61	78	0.6				
2018	WOR	AAA	24	0.98	1.65	87	0.2				
2019	WOR	AAA	25	1.53	4.60	108	0.4				
2019	BOS	MLB	25	1.41	3.86	124	-0.2	95.2	71.0%	25.4%	
2020	BAL	MLB	26	1.48	2.81	94	0.3	94.7	73.6%	22.5%	
2021 FS	BAL	MLB	27	1.49	5.15	110	0.0	94.9	72.7%	23.6%	45.8%
2021 DC	BAL	MLB	27	1.49	5.15	110	0.0	94.9	72.7%	23.6%	45.8%

Travis Lakins Sr., continued

Pitch Shape vs LHH

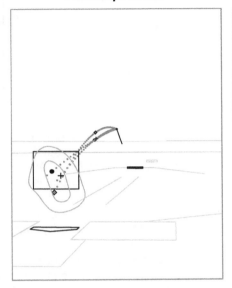

Pitch Shape vs RHH

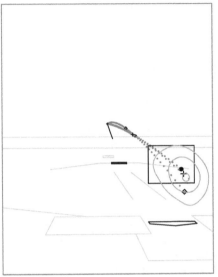

Type	Frequency	Velocity	H Movement	V Movement
● Fastball	31.7%	93.4 [103]	-3.9 [113]	-14.5 [102]
+ Cutter	41.9%	90.9 [116]	3.1 [107]	-22.1 [108]
▲ Changeup	3.2%	87.6 [110]	-13.1 [93]	-29.6 [94]
◇ Curveball	22.3%	80.6 [108]	10.2 [111]	-48.9 [99]

John Means LHP

Born: 04/24/93   Age: 28   Bats: L   Throws: L
Height: 6'3"   Weight: 230   Origin: Round 11, 2014 Draft (#331 overall)

YEAR	TEAM	LVL	AGE	W	L	SV	G	GS	IP	H	HR	BB/9	K/9	K	GB%	BABIP
2018	BOW	AA	25	1	4	0	8	7	46	43	6	2.5	8.0	41	37.1%	.282
2018	NOR	AAA	25	6	5	0	20	19	111^1	123	9	1.5	7.2	89	33.8%	.326
2018	BAL	MLB	25	0	0	0	1	0	3^1	6	1	0.0	10.8	4	25.0%	.455
2019	BAL	MLB	26	12	11	0	31	27	155	138	23	2.2	7.0	121	30.7%	.256
2020	BAL	MLB	27	2	4	0	10	10	43^2	36	12	1.4	8.7	42	43.9%	.216
2021 FS	BAL	MLB	28	10	8	0	26	26	150	138	27	2.2	8.1	134	36.3%	.271
2021 DC	BAL	MLB	28	9	8	0	29	27	145.7	134	26	2.2	8.1	130	36.3%	.271

Comparables: Andrew Suárez, Caleb Smith, Erick Fedde

It was a tale of two seasons for the Orioles' 2019 All-Star. He got off to a late start, coming out of Spring Camp 2.0 with some shoulder fatigue, struggled early on and then missed a few starts after his father passed away in mid August. But once he got into the groove of things in the seasons' second month (also its last month, idk if you saw but there was a Pandemic), he was back to 2019 John Means, but even better. The big story here was that his fastball velo jumped 2.1 miles per hour compared to the season before; the fourth biggest velocity leap in the bigs. He didn't throw the fastball any more often, but it generated 11% more swings and misses than 2019 and had an XBA under 2. His fastball went from a necessity to a legit weapon. It's pretty crazy. As an 11th round pick, he's already an astounding developmental success, and if he can piece 2019's cambio with 2020's heater he'll be a solid, postseason startable Big League pitcher for the next few years.

YEAR	TEAM	LVL	AGE	WHIP	ERA	DRA-	WARP	MPH	FB%	WHF	CSP
2018	BOW	AA	25	1.22	4.30	80	0.8				
2018	NOR	AAA	25	1.28	3.48	88	1.4				
2018	BAL	MLB	25	1.80	13.50	219	-0.2	91.6	37.9%	22.2%	
2019	BAL	MLB	26	1.14	3.60	94	1.9	93.6	50.7%	22.2%	
2020	BAL	MLB	27	0.98	4.53	105	0.3	95.5	52.3%	26.3%	
2021 FS	BAL	MLB	28	1.17	3.86	88	2.4	94.1	51.1%	23.4%	47.8%
2021 DC	BAL	MLB	28	1.17	3.86	88	2.2	94.1	51.1%	23.4%	47.8%

John Means, continued

Pitch Shape vs LHH	Pitch Shape vs RHH

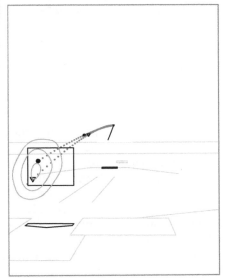 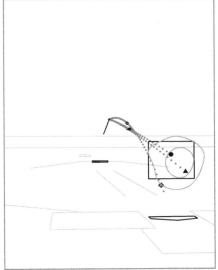

Type	Frequency	Velocity	H Movement	V Movement
● Fastball	52.3%	93.9 [104]	5.7 [105]	-10.8 [113]
▲ Changeup	24.7%	85 [99]	12 [99]	-19 [123]
▽ Slider	10.3%	86.6 [112]	-3.8 [95]	-26.9 [120]
◇ Curveball	12.6%	79.1 [102]	-12.3 [119]	-48.9 [99]

Tanner Scott   LHP

Born: 07/22/94   Age: 26   Bats: R   Throws: L
Height: 6'2"   Weight: 220   Origin: Round 6, 2014 Draft (#181 overall)

YEAR	TEAM	LVL	AGE	W	L	SV	G	GS	IP	H	HR	BB/9	K/9	K	GB%	BABIP
2018	NOR	AAA	23	0	1	0	10	0	12	10	0	6.8	9.8	13	55.2%	.357
2018	BAL	MLB	23	3	3	0	53	0	53¹	55	6	4.7	12.8	76	46.7%	.383
2019	NOR	AAA	24	3	4	7	30	0	45¹	35	2	3.0	11.3	57	55.9%	.303
2019	BAL	MLB	24	1	1	0	28	0	26¹	28	4	6.5	12.6	37	51.6%	.400
2020	BAL	MLB	25	0	0	1	25	0	20²	12	1	4.4	10.0	23	58.0%	.224
2021 FS	BAL	MLB	26	2	2	6	57	0	50	42	6	5.5	11.2	62	51.1%	.302
2021 DC	BAL	MLB	26	3	3	6	64	0	71.3	60	8	5.5	11.2	88	51.1%	.302

Comparables: José Alvarado, Keone Kela, Tyler Mahle

After a few years of inconsistent results, the 25-year-old finally put it together, evolving into the overpowering lefty world-crusher that overly optimistic O's fans always thought he could be. It's a pretty simple recipe for success: a bulkier Josh Hader without the hair, Andrew Miller with regular-sized limbs. In other words, it's elite fastball velocity and spin from the left side with one of the best wipeout sliders in the world. Granted, it was only a 20-inning sample, but Scott was actually better against opposite-handed hitters in 2020, thanks mostly to a slider that gained 200 RPM compared to where it was in 2019. The next questions for Scott are: (1) can he maintain this over a full season, and (2) can he do this in multi-inning outings? If 2021 answers yes to both questions, and that's a big if, Scott has a shot to be a top-10 reliever in baseball.

YEAR	TEAM	LVL	AGE	WHIP	ERA	DRA-	WARP	MPH	FB%	WHF	CSP
2018	NOR	AAA	23	1.58	0.75	74	0.2				
2018	BAL	MLB	23	1.56	5.40	63	1.3	98.8	55.4%	35.2%	
2019	NOR	AAA	24	1.10	2.98	50	1.7				
2019	BAL	MLB	24	1.78	4.78	92	0.2	97.8	58.7%	34.1%	
2020	BAL	MLB	25	1.06	1.31	73	0.5	98.2	61.5%	35.9%	
2021 FS	BAL	MLB	26	1.46	4.43	95	0.4	98.3	58.6%	35.1%	45.3%
2021 DC	BAL	MLB	26	1.46	4.43	95	0.5	98.3	58.6%	35.1%	45.3%

Tanner Scott, continued

Pitch Shape vs LHH

Pitch Shape vs RHH

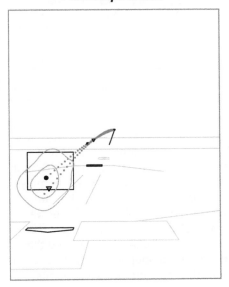
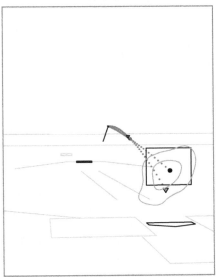

Type	Frequency	Velocity	H Movement	V Movement
● Fastball	59.8%	96.5 [113]	3.6 [115]	-13.3 [105]
▽ Slider	38.5%	88.3 [120]	-4.7 [98]	-32.3 [104]

Cole Sulser RHP

Born: 03/12/90   Age: 31   Bats: R   Throws: R
Height: 6'1"   Weight: 190   Origin: Round 25, 2013 Draft (#741 overall)

YEAR	TEAM	LVL	AGE	W	L	SV	G	GS	IP	H	HR	BB/9	K/9	K	GB%	BABIP
2018	AKR	AA	28	3	0	1	6	0	9	3	0	1.0	17.0	17	41.7%	.250
2018	COL	AAA	28	5	4	1	41	0	51²	52	4	2.8	13.6	78	34.7%	.410
2019	DUR	AAA	29	6	3	2	49	4	66	51	4	3.3	12.1	89	31.8%	.309
2019	TB	MLB	29	0	0	0	7	0	7¹	5	0	3.7	11.0	9	35.3%	.294
2020	BAL	MLB	30	1	5	5	19	0	22²	17	2	6.8	7.5	19	37.5%	.250
2021 FS	BAL	MLB	31	2	2	0	57	0	50	43	8	3.8	9.9	54	36.8%	.280
2021 DC	BAL	MLB	31	2	2	0	51	0	57	49	9	3.8	9.9	62	36.8%	.280

Comparables: Jacob Barnes, Andrew Kittredge, Richard Rodríguez

You can't spell C-O-L-E S-U-L-S-E-R without CLOSER. And that was the damn truth on the opening weekend when O's manager Brandon Hyde sent him out for a two-inning save against (what we thought at the time was) a good Boston lineup, and it worked. While there were some bumps along the way—namely the game he blew on July 30 when Aaron Judge hit one to Venus—July and August were going pretty nifty for the short-arming late-bloomer. Sulser was averaging a strikeout per inning and had an ERA under 3.50 on August 22. But back-to-back blown saves against Toronto at the end of August bumped the Proven Sulser out of the ninth inning, and his September was pretty forgettable. He still has above-average velocity, great fastball spin numbers and almost certainly a spot in the 2021 Orioles bullpen, but Baltimore might have to spell out Closer without Cole Sulser going forward.

YEAR	TEAM	LVL	AGE	WHIP	ERA	DRA-	WARP	MPH	FB%	WHF	CSP
2018	AKR	AA	28	0.44	0.00	50	0.3				
2018	COL	AAA	28	1.32	4.53	71	1.0				
2019	DUR	AAA	29	1.14	3.27	52	2.4				
2019	TB	MLB	29	1.09	0.00	87	0.1	94.5	63.8%	25.8%	
2020	BAL	MLB	30	1.50	5.56	117	0.0	95.1	57.5%	30.2%	
2021 FS	BAL	MLB	31	1.29	4.10	91	0.5	95.0	58.6%	29.4%	43.6%
2021 DC	BAL	MLB	31	1.29	4.10	91	0.6	95.0	58.6%	29.4%	43.6%

Cole Sulser, continued

Pitch Shape vs LHH

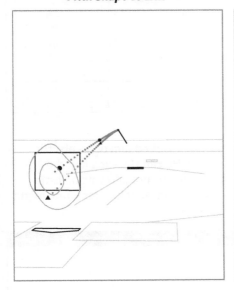

Pitch Shape vs RHH

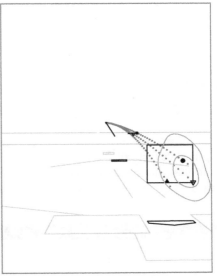

Type	Frequency	Velocity	H Movement	V Movement
● Fastball	57.3%	93.9 [104]	-9 [89]	-11.5 [111]
▲ Changeup	25.9%	85.8 [103]	-13.3 [92]	-24.4 [108]
▽ Slider	16.5%	87.6 [116]	3 [91]	-25 [125]

Dillon Tate   RHP

Born: 05/01/94   Age: 27   Bats: R   Throws: R
Height: 6'2"   Weight: 195   Origin: Round 1, 2015 Draft (#4 overall)

YEAR	TEAM	LVL	AGE	W	L	SV	G	GS	IP	H	HR	BB/9	K/9	K	GB%	BABIP
2018	TRN	AA	24	5	2	0	15	15	82²	67	7	2.7	8.2	75	48.1%	.263
2018	BOW	AA	24	2	3	0	7	7	40²	48	3	2.0	4.6	21	61.3%	.328
2019	BOW	AA	25	2	3	5	17	2	33²	28	4	2.4	8.0	30	49.0%	.264
2019	NOR	AAA	25	2	0	2	4	0	9	7	1	1.0	7.0	7	65.4%	.240
2019	BAL	MLB	25	0	2	0	16	0	21	18	3	3.9	8.6	20	61.0%	.268
2020	BAL	MLB	26	1	1	0	12	0	16²	9	1	2.7	7.6	14	51.2%	.190
2021 FS	BAL	MLB	27	2	2	0	57	0	50	48	6	3.8	8.1	44	51.3%	.293
2021 DC	BAL	MLB	27	3	3	0	64	0	57	55	7	3.8	8.1	51	51.3%	.293

Comparables: Spencer Turnbull, Rookie Davis, Sam Tuivailala

A former fourth-overall pick, Tate's journey has robbed him of his electric upper-90s fastball and his chance to be a starter. He can still sling it in the mid-90s, though, and he was effective at that velocity, not allowing an extra-base hit on the heater last season. By not dwelling on what he's lost, Tate might have secured himself a career as a middle reliever.

YEAR	TEAM	LVL	AGE	WHIP	ERA	DRA-	WARP	MPH	FB%	WHF	CSP
2018	TRN	AA	24	1.11	3.38	66	2.1				
2018	BOW	AA	24	1.40	5.75	90	0.5				
2019	BOW	AA	25	1.10	3.48	94	0.0				
2019	NOR	AAA	25	0.89	2.00	62	0.3				
2019	BAL	MLB	25	1.29	6.43	95	0.2	95.8	56.6%	21.6%	
2020	BAL	MLB	26	0.84	3.24	87	0.3	96.9	57.9%	25.0%	
2021 FS	BAL	MLB	27	1.40	4.65	100	0.2	96.4	57.3%	23.5%	46.6%
2021 DC	BAL	MLB	27	1.40	4.65	100	0.3	96.4	57.3%	23.5%	46.6%

Dillon Tate, continued

Pitch Shape vs LHH   ### Pitch Shape vs RHH

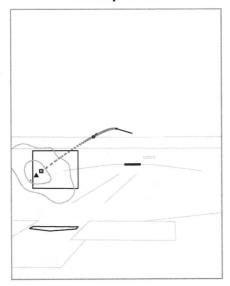 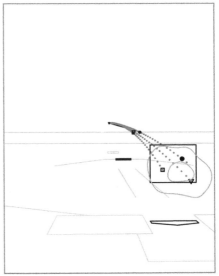

Type	Frequency	Velocity	H Movement	V Movement
● Fastball	22.8%	95.2 [108]	-9.1 [88]	-15.4 [100]
□ Sinker	35.1%	93.9 [108]	-14.2 [92]	-22.7 [93]
▲ Changeup	16.1%	83.8 [95]	-13.8 [89]	-28 [99]
▽ Slider	26.0%	85.5 [107]	2.3 [89]	-30.3 [110]

Cesar Valdez RHP

Born: 03/17/85   Age: 36   Bats: R   Throws: R
Height: 6'2"   Weight: 200   Origin: International Free Agent, 2005

YEAR	TEAM	LVL	AGE	W	L	SV	G	GS	IP	H	HR	BB/9	K/9	K	GB%	BABIP
2018	TAB	AAA	33	1	3	0	7	7	30^1	53	3	1.8	6.8	23	42.0%	.435
2018	YUC	AAA	33	5	0	0	6	6	36^1	39	0	1.2	9.2	37	62.4%	.358
2019	YUC	AAA	34	15	2	0	23	23	147^2	140	6	1.0	7.4	122	56.6%	.311
2020	BAL	MLB	35	1	1	3	9	0	14^1	7	0	1.9	7.5	12	52.6%	.184
2021 FS	BAL	MLB	36	2	2	0	57	0	50	49	8	2.1	7.3	40	47.8%	.284
2021 DC	BAL	MLB	36	8	5	0	64	6	75.7	75	12	2.1	7.3	61	47.8%	.284

Comparables: Matt Albers, Andrew Miller, Junior Guerra

Coming into the year, the 35-year-old Valdez had not pitched in the majors since 2017 with Toronto, had no track record of success in the bigs and a fastball in the mid-80s. After proving himself at the alternate site, he got the call toward the end of August and spent 14 1/3 innings absolutely carving out of the Orioles bullpen. It was all thanks to his "dead fish" changeup, a mythical offering that Valdez threw a whopping 83 percent of the time, baffling hitters to the tune of a .164 batting average against. He uses it like a knuckleball, floating it all around and below the zone with incredible touch. Scream small sample size all you want, but this is the best trick pitch in baseball right now. Maybe this is a real repeatable gimmick and the longtime journeyman (he's spent time in Taiwan, Mexico, the Dominican Republic, Venezuela and Puerto Rico) has an R.A. Dickey-like five years ahead of him. He pitched well enough to earn a second season making pitches disappear just beneath opposing hitters' bats.

YEAR	TEAM	LVL	AGE	WHIP	ERA	DRA-	WARP	MPH	FB%	WHF	CSP
2018	TAB	AAA	33	1.95	5.93						
2018	YUC	AAA	33	1.21	2.48						
2019	YUC	AAA	34	1.06	2.26						
2020	BAL	MLB	35	0.70	1.26	85	0.2	86.9	15.7%	30.3%	
2021 FS	BAL	MLB	36	1.23	4.05	92	0.5	86.9	15.7%	30.3%	47.3%
2021 DC	BAL	MLB	36	1.23	4.05	92	0.7	86.9	15.7%	30.3%	47.3%

Cesar Valdez, continued

Pitch Shape vs LHH

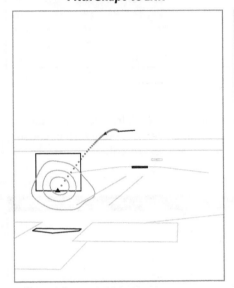

Pitch Shape vs RHH

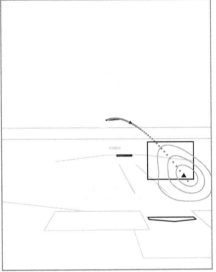

Type	Frequency	Velocity	H Movement	V Movement
● Fastball	6.3%	85.3 [77]	-13.4 [68]	-24.3 [74]
□ Sinker	9.4%	85.6 [65]	-16.2 [77]	-34 [56]
▲ Changeup	83.2%	77.8 [71]	-9.3 [113]	-45.1 [52]

Baltimore Orioles 2021

Asher Wojciechowski   RHP
Born: 12/21/88   Age: 32   Bats: R   Throws: R
Height: 6'4"   Weight: 235   Origin: Round 1, 2010 Draft (#41 overall)

YEAR	TEAM	LVL	AGE	W	L	SV	G	GS	IP	H	HR	BB/9	K/9	K	GB%	BABIP
2018	CHA	AAA	29	0	5	0	6	6	34²	40	12	1.3	9.6	37	26.2%	.308
2018	NOR	AAA	29	5	4	0	19	12	84²	68	14	3.4	9.5	89	29.6%	.256
2019	COL	AAA	30	8	2	0	15	15	84²	67	19	3.3	8.7	82	27.0%	.229
2019	BAL	MLB	30	4	8	0	17	16	82¹	80	17	3.1	8.7	80	29.9%	.279
2020	BAL	MLB	31	1	3	0	10	7	37	45	11	3.6	7.5	31	30.0%	.315
2021 FS	*BAL*	*MLB*	*32*	*2*	*3*	*0*	*57*	*0*	*50*	*50*	*11*	*3.4*	*8.1*	*45*	*29.6%*	*.278*

Comparables: Chris Rusin, Tyler Cloyd, David Huff

Wojciechowski spent this summer challenging ESPN's Adrian Wojnarowski for who could serve up the most bombs. He struggled even in that regard because he didn't stay in the rotation long enough to pose a real threat.

YEAR	TEAM	LVL	AGE	WHIP	ERA	DRA-	WARP	MPH	FB%	WHF	CSP
2018	CHA	AAA	29	1.30	7.01	94	0.3				
2018	NOR	AAA	29	1.18	3.51	88	1.1				
2019	COL	AAA	30	1.16	3.61	88	2.0				
2019	BAL	MLB	30	1.31	4.92	111	0.3	93.4	53.9%	26.1%	
2020	BAL	MLB	31	1.62	6.81	157	-0.8	92.6	46.1%	25.6%	
2021 FS	*BAL*	*MLB*	*32*	*1.38*	*5.30*	*114*	*-0.1*	*93.0*	*50.7%*	*25.9%*	*46.0%*

Asher Wojciechowski, continued

Pitch Shape vs LHH

Pitch Shape vs RHH

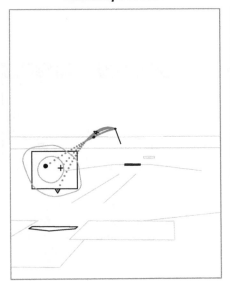
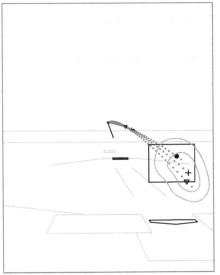

Type	Frequency	Velocity	H Movement	V Movement
● Fastball	46.1%	91 [95]	-5 [108]	-13.5 [105]
+ Cutter	21.8%	85.8 [84]	4 [113]	-27.6 [87]
▲ Changeup	5.2%	84.6 [98]	-8.1 [119]	-22.7 [113]
▽ Slider	26.9%	78.2 [74]	13.5 [131]	-42.8 [74]

PLAYER COMMENTS WITHOUT GRAPHS

Rylan Bannon 2B

Born: 04/22/96   Age: 25   Bats: R   Throws: R
Height: 5'8"   Weight: 180   Origin: Round 8, 2017 Draft (#250 overall)

YEAR	TEAM	LVL	AGE	PA	R	2B	3B	HR	RBI	BB	K	SB	CS	AVG/OBP/SLG
2018	RC	HI-A	22	403	58	17	6	20	61	59	103	4	4	.296/.402/.559
2018	BOW	AA	22	122	16	6	0	2	11	22	24	0	0	.204/.344/.327
2019	BOW	AA	23	444	45	22	4	8	42	47	72	8	4	.255/.345/.394
2019	NOR	AAA	23	90	18	10	0	3	17	3	14	0	1	.317/.344/.549
2021 FS	BAL	MLB	25	600	68	24	1	17	60	53	162	1	1	.224/.302/.371
2021 DC	BAL	MLB	25	66	7	2	0	1	6	5	17	0	0	.224/.302/.371

Comparables: Jefry Marte, Taylor Green, James Darnell

As a 5-foot-8 utility infielder who hasn't played any shortstop and isn't dynamic on defense, Bannon has to show he can hit high-level pitching to be more than a bench bat. There've been flashes of raw power and he held his own in Triple-A in 2019, but struggled in the Fall League afterwards. He should see the majors in 2021.

YEAR	TEAM	LVL	AGE	PA	DRC+	BABIP	BRR	FRAA	WARP
2018	RC	HI-A	22	403	160	.367	0.0	3B(54): 2.9, 2B(22): 0.2	2.9
2018	BOW	AA	22	122	99	.243	-1.4	2B(30): -0.9, 3B(2): -0.1	-0.1
2019	BOW	AA	23	444	124	.294	-0.4	3B(69): 1.8, 2B(38): 1.4	2.8
2019	NOR	AAA	23	90	119	.338	-0.3	3B(20): 3.1	0.7
2021 FS	BAL	MLB	25	600	84	.289	-0.7	2B 0, 3B 1	0.2
2021 DC	BAL	MLB	25	66	84	.289	-0.1	2B 0, 3B 0	0.0

Chris Davis   1B

Born: 03/17/86   Age: 35   Bats: L   Throws: R
Height: 6'3"   Weight: 245   Origin: Round 5, 2006 Draft (#148 overall)

YEAR	TEAM	LVL	AGE	PA	R	2B	3B	HR	RBI	BB	K	SB	CS	AVG/OBP/SLG
2018	BAL	MLB	32	522	40	12	0	16	49	41	192	2	0	.168/.243/.296
2019	BAL	MLB	33	352	26	9	0	12	36	39	139	0	0	.179/.276/.326
2020	BAL	MLB	34	55	3	3	0	0	1	3	17	0	0	.115/.164/.173
2021 FS	BAL	MLB	35	600	63	20	1	20	57	67	227	1	1	.187/.288/.344
2021 DC	BAL	MLB	35	218	22	7	0	7	20	24	82	0	0	.187/.288/.344

Comparables: Mike Napoli, Tony Clark, Dave Kingman

Davis' infamous 0-for-54 start to the 2019 season was big news. For the final 20 plate appearances or so of that streak, the whole baseball community was tuned in to every start as the Slugger Formerly Known as Chris Davis flailed his way into the history books. Davis became the sport's biggest meme, its most tragic punchline. Eventually he roped a single into left field off Rick Porcello, and suddenly he was merely the worst hitter in baseball. The baseball world had moved on.

Davis was just as inept in 2020. No one cared. Watching him hit gave off the vibe of living among the ruins of ancient Greece: you know something grand once stood there, something awe-inspiring, but now you're just sleeping on rocks. It must be emphasized that he was once a majestic baseball thing, a mountain with forearms of stone, capable of depositing baseballs into new zip codes. To fall like he's fallen, you've got to reach a certain height in the first place. He was basically phantom IL'ed for the last month-plus of the season, tallying only three at-bats after August 18th. There's been chatter about a buyout, some muttering about how Crush has played his last game, despite the two years left on his contract. Who knows what the future holds, but if this truly is the end, a hefty kudos to a man who reached unimaginable highs and unwatchable lows, but through it all went back out there each day and tried to smack the crap out of the ball.

YEAR	TEAM	LVL	AGE	PA	DRC+	BABIP	BRR	FRAA	WARP
2018	BAL	MLB	32	522	56	.237	-4.6	1B(116): -5.4	-3.2
2019	BAL	MLB	33	352	64	.270	0.7	1B(97): -4.6, RF(1): -0.6, P(1): -0.0	-1.5
2020	BAL	MLB	34	55	65	.171	0.1	1B(15): 1.6	-0.1
2021 FS	BAL	MLB	35	600	72	.282	-0.8	1B -2, RF 0	-1.6
2021 DC	BAL	MLB	35	218	72	.282	-0.3	1B -1	-0.6

Yusniel Diaz   RF

Born: 10/07/96   Age: 24   Bats: R   Throws: R
Height: 6'1"   Weight: 210   Origin: International Free Agent, 2015

YEAR	TEAM	LVL	AGE	PA	R	2B	3B	HR	RBI	BB	K	SB	CS	AVG/OBP/SLG
2018	TUL	AA	21	264	36	10	4	6	30	41	39	8	8	.314/.428/.477
2018	BOW	AA	21	152	23	5	1	5	15	18	28	4	5	.239/.329/.403
2019	FRE	HI-A	22	25	0	0	0	0	2	3	7	0	0	.273/.360/.273
2019	BOW	AA	22	322	45	19	4	11	53	32	67	0	3	.262/.335/.472
2021 FS	BAL	MLB	24	600	70	24	2	18	63	54	161	5	4	.235/.308/.390
2021 DC	BAL	MLB	24	133	15	5	0	4	14	12	35	1	1	.235/.308/.390

Comparables: Rene Tosoni, Michael Reed, Domonic Brown

We've reached the point where Díaz's prospect fame almost certainly over-hypes his prospect status. When you smack two dingers in the Futures Game and then become the headliner in a Manny Machado trade days later, your name will hop on the map. And when you're a ripped Cuban dude whose name starts with a Y who got a bunch of money as an amateur ... ooh boy. But in his current state, Díaz has true tweener potential. He's not long for center field (especially in an org with Austin Hays and Cedric Mullins), and evaluators are concerned he won't hit for enough power for the bat to play in a corner. Díaz has a good approach at the plate (check his 14 percent walk rate in LIDOM last year), but the exit velocity numbers are closer to good than great, which just puts a limit on the ceiling and a ton of pressure on the bat. He'll get a a chance in the bigs in 2021 and could be a solid big leaguer, but odds are he's not the super-hyped Machado headliner he once was.

YEAR	TEAM	LVL	AGE	PA	DRC+	BABIP	BRR	FRAA	WARP
2018	TUL	AA	21	264	159	.360	1.8	CF(29): -1.7, RF(28): -1.6, LF(2): -0.5	1.5
2018	BOW	AA	21	152	96	.267	-0.5	RF(29): 0.3, CF(6): -0.5	-0.1
2019	FRE	HI-A	22	25	88	.400	-0.6	CF(5): -0.4	-0.1
2019	BOW	AA	22	322	150	.303	0.6	RF(53): 1.4, CF(5): 0.3, LF(2): 0.1	2.5
2021 FS	BAL	MLB	24	600	89	.300	-0.1	LF 6, CF 0	1.2
2021 DC	BAL	MLB	24	133	89	.300	0.0	LF 1	0.2

Gunnar Henderson SS

Born: 06/29/01   Age: 20   Bats: L   Throws: R
Height: 6'3"   Weight: 195   Origin: Round 2, 2019 Draft (#42 overall)

YEAR	TEAM	LVL	AGE	PA	R	2B	3B	HR	RBI	BB	K	SB	CS	AVG/OBP/SLG
2019	ORI	ROK	18	121	21	5	2	1	11	11	28	2	2	.259/.331/.370
2021 FS	BAL	MLB	20	600	42	17	2	8	47	32	215	5	4	.181/.230/.268

Comparables: Rey Navarro, Isan Díaz, Gavin Cecchini

A tall shortstop with big power who will probably slide over to third base sooner rather than later, Henderson is trying to become the first Gunnar in big-league history. Taken with the compensation-round pick after Adley Rutschman went first overall, Henderson went to the Gulf Coast league in 2019 to get his toes into the professional baseball water. Then during the pandemic, the 19-year-old scored a surprising invite to the Orioles' alternate site to face off against baseballers half a decade his elder. Unsurprisingly, he struggled. The BP prospect maestros ranked ol' Gunnar 11th on their team list, but if he shows up in Low-A and rakes, he'll leap up into the top 4 or 5. There's also a chance the swing-and-miss issues manifest themselves further, forcing us to wait even longer for baseball's first Gunnar.

YEAR	TEAM	LVL	AGE	PA	DRC+	BABIP	BRR	FRAA	WARP
2019	ORI	ROK	18	121		.338			
2021 FS	BAL	MLB	20	600	35	.274	0.3	SS -3	-3.4

Jahmai Jones 2B

Born: 08/04/97   Age: 23   Bats: R   Throws: R
Height: 6'0"   Weight: 204   Origin: Round 2, 2015 Draft (#70 overall)

YEAR	TEAM	LVL	AGE	PA	R	2B	3B	HR	RBI	BB	K	SB	CS	AVG/OBP/SLG
2018	IE	HI-A	20	347	47	10	5	8	35	43	63	13	3	.235/.338/.383
2018	MOB	AA	20	212	33	10	4	2	20	24	51	11	1	.245/.335/.375
2019	MOB	AA	21	544	66	22	3	5	50	50	109	9	11	.234/.308/.324
2020	LAA	MLB	22	7	2	0	0	0	1	0	2	0	0	.429/.429/.429
2021 FS	BAL	MLB	23	600	59	22	2	14	59	47	160	9	5	.219/.289/.350
2021 DC	BAL	MLB	23	62	6	2	0	1	6	4	16	0	1	.219/.289/.350

Comparables: Luis Valbuena, Eddie Rosario, Abraham Toro

Forget keeping up with the Joneses. A number of Angels prospects have leapfrogged the infielder in recent years, while he changed positions and never really brought everything together in the batter's box. Jones debuted in the majors last year, but it wasn't enough to obfuscate the feeling of his prospect potential having stalled. Now he's got to figure out how to keep up with everyone else.

YEAR	TEAM	LVL	AGE	PA	DRC+	BABIP	BRR	FRAA	WARP
2018	IE	HI-A	20	347	111	.272	1.5	2B(70): -6.9	-0.1
2018	MOB	AA	20	212	103	.323	-1.5	2B(45): -1.7	-0.1
2019	MOB	AA	21	544	79	.288	2.3	2B(110): 14.4, CF(7): 0.3, LF(4): -0.6	2.3
2020	LAA	MLB	22	7	89	.600	-0.1	2B(2): -0.0	0.0
2021 FS	*BAL*	*MLB*	*23*	*600*	*75*	*.284*	*0.6*	*2B 1, LF 0*	*0.1*
2021 DC	*BAL*	*MLB*	*23*	*62*	*75*	*.284*	*0.1*	*2B 0*	*0.0*

Heston Kjerstad OF
Born: 02/12/99   Age: 22   Bats: L   Throws: R
Height: 6'3"   Weight: 220   Origin: Round 1, 2020 Draft (#2 overall)

The Orioles surprised prognosticators by taking Kjerstad second overall. But it's not like Elias and Co. snagged a schlub off your local ball field—Kjerstad was on track to be a Golden Spikes finalist. While he lacks the ceiling and premium defensive position you might expect from a no. 2 overall pick, he can really hit. He demolished the best conference in college baseball in his first two seasons and was hitting around .450 with six homers in 16 games before the pandemic happened. His freshman swing was pretty choppy, but he really smoothed things out over his college career without compromising production. He has impressive bat control, with great bat speed and big power. Unless he gets too big and loses speed, he should be able to handle a corner outfield spot. He's a bit overeager at the plate, but who among us wasn't when we were 21? The ideal outcome looks kinda like a taller, harder-to-spell Michael Conforto.

Trey Mancini RF

Born: 03/18/92 Age: 29 Bats: R Throws: R
Height: 6'4" Weight: 230 Origin: Round 8, 2013 Draft (#249 overall)

YEAR	TEAM	LVL	AGE	PA	R	2B	3B	HR	RBI	BB	K	SB	CS	AVG/OBP/SLG
2018	BAL	MLB	26	636	69	23	3	24	58	44	153	0	1	.242/.299/.416
2019	BAL	MLB	27	679	106	38	2	35	97	63	142	1	0	.291/.364/.535
2021 FS	BAL	MLB	29	600	79	27	1	27	73	47	152	0	1	.260/.327/.466
2021 DC	BAL	MLB	29	491	65	22	1	22	60	38	124	0	1	.260/.327/.466

Comparables: Geoff Jenkins, Kevin Reimer, Marcell Ozuna

After a classic "great hitter on bad team" performance in 2019, Mancini missed the entire 2020 season after doctors discovered a tumor in his colon during spring training. Mancini was diagnosed with stage 3 colon cancer and underwent chemotherapy. He finished up treatments in late September, and O's GM Mike Elias indicated that the club expects Mancini to be ready to go next season. One of two remaining members from Baltimore's last postseason team in 2016 (*sigh* Chris Davis is the other), Mancini could be the only guy to bridge the gap between two different eras of good Baltimore teams. Don't forget there was a good reason he was the only Oriole you'd heard of—Mancini can flat-out hit. He had a higher OPS in 2019 than Bryce Harper, DJ LeMahieu and Max Muncy. Whatever 2021 brings for him on the field, the important thing is that Mancini won his showdown with cancer and appears to be on the road back to the diamond.

YEAR	TEAM	LVL	AGE	PA	DRC+	BABIP	BRR	FRAA	WARP
2018	BAL	MLB	26	636	91	.285	0.5	LF(98): 4.5, 1B(47): 2.7	1.5
2019	BAL	MLB	27	679	120	.326	-0.9	RF(87): -3.6, 1B(56): 1.7, LF(6): -0.3	2.8
2021 FS	BAL	MLB	29	600	110	.314	-0.8	1B 1, LF 0	2.0
2021 DC	BAL	MLB	29	491	110	.314	-0.7	1B 1	1.4

Richie Martin SS

Born: 12/22/94 Age: 26 Bats: R Throws: R
Height: 5'11" Weight: 190 Origin: Round 1, 2015 Draft (#20 overall)

YEAR	TEAM	LVL	AGE	PA	R	2B	3B	HR	RBI	BB	K	SB	CS	AVG/OBP/SLG
2018	MID	AA	23	509	68	29	8	6	42	44	86	25	10	.300/.368/.439
2019	BAL	MLB	24	309	29	8	3	6	23	14	83	10	1	.208/.260/.322
2021 FS	BAL	MLB	26	600	58	20	2	12	50	41	163	12	4	.209/.280/.323
2021 DC	BAL	MLB	26	29	2	0	0	0	2	1	7	0	0	.209/.280/.323

Comparables: Felix Escalona, Tom Matchick, Benji Gil

A stellar glove and speedy shoes have always been stowed safely in Martin's locker. A 2020 spent rehabbing a broken wrist hopefully gave him some time to search for his missing bat.

YEAR	TEAM	LVL	AGE	PA	DRC+	BABIP	BRR	FRAA	WARP
2018	MID	AA	23	509	119	.357	-0.3	SS(96): 9.1, 2B(21): 1.0	3.0
2019	BAL	MLB	24	309	50	.272	-0.9	SS(117): -0.8	-0.7
2021 FS	BAL	MLB	26	600	66	.276	0.7	SS 1, 2B 0	-0.6
2021 DC	BAL	MLB	26	29	66	.276	0.0	SS 0	0.0

Ryan McKenna   CF

Born: 02/14/97   Age: 24   Bats: R   Throws: R
Height: 5'11"   Weight: 185   Origin: Round 4, 2015 Draft (#133 overall)

YEAR	TEAM	LVL	AGE	PA	R	2B	3B	HR	RBI	BB	K	SB	CS	AVG/OBP/SLG
2018	FRE	HI-A	21	301	60	18	2	8	37	37	45	5	6	.377/.467/.556
2018	BOW	AA	21	250	35	8	2	3	16	29	56	4	1	.239/.341/.338
2019	BOW	AA	22	567	78	26	6	9	54	59	121	25	11	.232/.321/.365
2021 FS	BAL	MLB	24	600	65	22	1	13	54	52	174	9	4	.218/.296/.343
2021 DC	BAL	MLB	24	33	3	1	0	0	3	2	9	0	0	.218/.296/.343

Comparables: Rey Fuentes, Michael Bourn, Brian Goodwin

With no minor-league season in 2020, we're forced to read into team decisions to determine what is up with prospects. McKenna, who spent all of 2019 in Double-A, figured to at least get a taste in the majors. Instead, he spent the whole year down at the alternate site. That probably had something to do with service-time tricks, as well as Cedric Mullins and Anthony Santander being way better than expected. The takeaway:even though McKenna remains a promising prospect who can play center and show average power, his bat wasn't electric enough in 2019 or 2020 to force a call-up. He's more physical than you'd expect from a 5-foot-11, 180-pound frame, and all his tools grade out around average. McKenna is almost certainly due for a debut in 2021, but he might find playing time tough to come by depending on how Mullins and Austin Hays (two other center fielders ahead of him on the pecking order) perform.

YEAR	TEAM	LVL	AGE	PA	DRC+	BABIP	BRR	FRAA	WARP
2018	FRE	HI-A	21	301	210	.436	2.5	CF(64): -6.2, LF(2): -0.2	3.4
2018	BOW	AA	21	250	90	.312	2.6	CF(55): 3.4, RF(3): 2.1, LF(2): -0.4	0.9
2019	BOW	AA	22	567	111	.287	1.9	CF(98): -4.1, LF(19): 0.6, RF(11): 0.9	2.3
2021 FS	BAL	MLB	24	600	76	.296	0.2	CF 7, LF 0	0.8
2021 DC	BAL	MLB	24	33	76	.296	0.0	CF 0	0.0

Adley Rutschman   C

Born: 02/06/98   Age: 23   Bats: S   Throws: R
Height: 6'2"   Weight: 220   Origin: Round 1, 2019 Draft (#1 overall)

YEAR	TEAM	LVL	AGE	PA	R	2B	3B	HR	RBI	BB	K	SB	CS	AVG/OBP/SLG
2019	ORI	ROK	21	16	3	0	0	1	3	2	2	1	0	.143/.250/.357
2019	ABD	SS	21	92	11	7	1	1	15	12	16	0	0	.325/.413/.481
2019	DEL	LO-A	21	47	5	1	0	2	8	6	9	0	0	.154/.261/.333
2021 FS	BAL	MLB	23	600	60	22	1	13	54	42	168	1	1	.210/.272/.331
2021 DC	BAL	MLB	23	66	6	2	0	1	6	4	18	0	0	.210/.272/.331

Comparables: Lucas Duda, Stuart Turner, Trey Mancini

If you're going to carry the future of a franchise on your shoulders, they might as well be enormous shoulders. Good thing Rutschman is built like a

YEAR	TEAM	P. COUNT	FRM RUNS	BLK RUNS	THRW RUNS	TOT RUNS
2019	DEL	769			0.1	0.0

refrigerator. What's in the fridge? Oh, only the best catching prospect in baseball. He's got a smooth, powerful swing with natural lift from both sides of the plate, he's a well above-average defender who relishes the finer points of handling a pitching staff and he once even scaled a redwood tree in a single bound to save an elderly lady stuck at the top. If it feels like Rutschman is Superman, a thicc prince who was promised, well … yeah. The cancelled minor-league season only extended the honeymoon between Orioles fans and Rutschman. The fans are now past month 20 of emotionally hinging their sports dreams to a baby-faced 22-year-old from Oregon who has only played 37 professional baseball games. It should be noted that for many Orioles fans, a Matt Wieters–shaped cloud hangs over the entire Adley Rutschman Experience. That's unfair to Rutschman (and probably Wieters), but every Orioles fan carries with them the ghosts of Franchise-Altering Catching Prospects Past. That lurking shadow—and the service time tricks that will most likely push back a debut to 2022—are the only worries here. This is what the no. 1 catcher in baseball looks like, and if a few things break right, he might be even better than that.

YEAR	TEAM	LVL	AGE	PA	DRC+	BABIP	BRR	FRAA	WARP
2019	ORI	ROK	21	16		.091			
2019	ABD	SS	21	92	177	.387	-0.1	C(8): -0.2	0.8
2019	DEL	LO-A	21	47	84	.138	0.1	C(6): 0.1	0.1
2021 FS	BAL	MLB	23	600	66	.278	-0.7	C 0	-0.2
2021 DC	BAL	MLB	23	66	66	.278	-0.1	C 0	0.0

Yolmer Sánchez 2B

Born: 06/29/92   Age: 29   Bats: S   Throws: R
Height: 5'8"   Weight: 205   Origin: International Free Agent, 2009

YEAR	TEAM	LVL	AGE	PA	R	2B	3B	HR	RBI	BB	K	SB	CS	AVG/OBP/SLG
2018	CHW	MLB	26	662	62	34	10	8	55	49	138	14	6	.242/.306/.372
2019	CHW	MLB	27	555	59	20	4	2	43	44	117	5	4	.252/.318/.321
2020	CHW	MLB	28	21	7	3	0	1	1	5	5	0	0	.312/.476/.688
2021 FS	BAL	MLB	29	600	61	25	3	12	54	44	142	8	5	.233/.298/.362
2021 DC	BAL	MLB	29	484	49	20	3	10	44	35	115	7	4	.233/.298/.362

Comparables: Randy Velarde, Greg Litton, Nick Green

Despite being just 28 years young, Sánchez has been playing professional baseball since 2009, plenty of time to become grizzled. And as a slick-fielding second baseman without power and only average contact ability, he's been around long enough to feel the ground of the game move underneath his feet. Second base defense has been devalued enough that no one was surprised to see Sánchez non-tendered after (deservedly) winning the Gold Glove in 2019, or settle for a minor league deal in the offseason. Veteran players have been devalued that it was further unsurprising that the Giants no longer had at-bats to issue to him when the schedule shrank to 60 games, so he eventually ended 2020 back with the White Sox like he never left. But like most tales when someone is brought back to life unnaturally, it didn't feel right. Sánchez didn't make Mickey Mouse ears to his son after hits, he didn't dunk Gatorade on his head during the pandemic, and even the dyed blonde streaks in his hair seemed tamer. He is only 28, but he has experienced the baseball world now, and while he will survive for a bit longer, his naïveté did not.

YEAR	TEAM	LVL	AGE	PA	DRC+	BABIP	BRR	FRAA	WARP
2018	CHW	MLB	26	662	80	.300	0.7	3B(141): -1.2, 2B(9): 0.2, SS(4): -0.3	0.7
2019	CHW	MLB	27	555	77	.324	0.2	2B(149): 19.0	2.1
2020	CHW	MLB	28	21	110	.400	-0.1	3B(5): -0.1, SS(3): 0.1, 2B(1): -0.0	0.1
2021 FS	BAL	MLB	29	600	80	.293	0.5	2B 5, SS 0	0.5
2021 DC	BAL	MLB	29	484	80	.293	0.4	2B 4, SS 0	0.7

Chance Sisco C

Born: 02/24/95   Age: 26   Bats: L   Throws: R
Height: 6'2"   Weight: 195   Origin: Round 2, 2013 Draft (#61 overall)

YEAR	TEAM	LVL	AGE	PA	R	2B	3B	HR	RBI	BB	K	SB	CS	AVG/OBP/SLG
2018	NOR	AAA	23	151	22	5	0	3	12	16	36	0	0	.242/.344/.352
2018	BAL	MLB	23	184	13	8	0	2	16	13	66	1	0	.181/.288/.269
2019	NOR	AAA	24	196	31	10	0	10	37	20	44	0	0	.292/.388/.530
2019	BAL	MLB	24	198	29	7	0	8	20	22	61	0	1	.210/.333/.395
2020	BAL	MLB	25	121	11	4	0	4	10	17	41	0	0	.214/.364/.378
2021 FS	BAL	MLB	26	600	71	19	1	21	63	64	190	0	1	.220/.328/.386
2021 DC	BAL	MLB	26	290	34	9	0	10	30	31	92	0	0	.220/.328/.386

Comparables: Andrew Knapp, Andrew Susac, John Russell

There are two positive outcomes for Sisco, neither of which really came to the fore in 2020. Either he needs to get more consistent behind the plate, or his bat needs to take another leap forward if he wants to be a 1B/DH type. Ater a hot August, Sisco came down hard in September and finished the year with very similar numbers to his average, yet uninspiring 2019.

YEAR	TEAM	P. COUNT	FRM RUNS	BLK RUNS	THRW RUNS	TOT RUNS
2018	BAL	6559	-2.2	0.3	-0.1	-1.9
2018	NOR	5320	-1.3	0.0	-0.8	-2.0
2019	BAL	6734	-9.6	-0.7	-0.5	-10.7
2019	NOR	5154	-1.8	0.3	-0.8	-2.4
2020	BAL	3179	-5.0	-0.9	0.1	-5.8
2021	BAL	9620	-9.2	-1.6	-0.1	-10.8
2021	BAL	9620	-9.2	-0.9	-0.1	-10.1

The one notable feature of his season was that he barreled balls at a pretty impressive rate (12.3 percent), which would have slotted him in between Christian Yelich and George Springer had Sisco qualified. There's nothing dynamic about Sisco's game. He's as electric as a power outage, but he's probably an average, if unremarkable hitter. That'll play behind the plate if he gets better defensively or if robots take over the strike zone. Otherwise, he'll need to start hitting the ball harder to nail down a long-term role in Baltimore once Adley the Chosen arrives.

YEAR	TEAM	LVL	AGE	PA	DRC+	BABIP	BRR	FRAA	WARP
2018	NOR	AAA	23	151	112	.308	-1.1	C(37): -2.8	0.3
2018	BAL	MLB	23	184	57	.293	-1.3	C(55): -2.8	-0.5
2019	NOR	AAA	24	196	131	.339	0.1	C(35): -3.3	1.2
2019	BAL	MLB	24	198	91	.276	0.1	C(52): -11.1, 1B(1): -0.0	-0.3
2020	BAL	MLB	25	121	100	.321	-1.1	C(26): -0.2	-0.3
2021 FS	BAL	MLB	26	600	96	.304	-0.8	C -16, 1B 0	0.4
2021 DC	BAL	MLB	26	290	96	.304	-0.4	C -10	-0.1

DJ Stewart   RF

Born: 11/30/93   Age: 27   Bats: L   Throws: R
Height: 6'0"   Weight: 230   Origin: Round 1, 2015 Draft (#25 overall)

YEAR	TEAM	LVL	AGE	PA	R	2B	3B	HR	RBI	BB	K	SB	CS	AVG/OBP/SLG
2018	NOR	AAA	24	490	59	24	2	12	55	54	103	11	4	.235/.329/.387
2018	BAL	MLB	24	47	8	3	0	3	10	4	12	2	1	.250/.340/.550
2019	NOR	AAA	25	277	42	19	2	12	47	38	51	5	4	.291/.396/.548
2019	BAL	MLB	25	142	15	6	0	4	15	14	26	1	2	.238/.317/.381
2020	BAL	MLB	26	112	13	2	0	7	15	20	38	0	0	.193/.355/.455
2021 FS	BAL	MLB	27	600	73	22	2	23	66	71	175	7	3	.214/.320/.400
2021 DC	BAL	MLB	27	333	40	12	1	13	36	39	97	3	2	.214/.320/.400

Comparables: Lyle Mouton, Chris Snelling, Rob Mackowiak

What a weird year. After going hitless in his first 22 trips to the plate, Stewart got sent back to the *OMINOUS DUH DUH DUH DUH* *alternate site*. But upon returning to Baltimore in early September, he looked like a whole new ballplayer, smacking six homers in his first six games back. It was a glorious week, one for the annals of franchise history. But the wind changed one last time as Stewart finished the year with an arctic final two weeks. In conclusion, Stewart is a land of contrasts. Especially considering he made the exact changes we recommended back in 2017, advising him to "find some power and a sustainable on-base percentage." Last year, Stewart was an underwhelming corner outfielder. Now, he has an outside shot to be Outfield Max Muncy. It's not clear if he's actually a good baseball player just yet, but he's added some intrigue to the profile—something we should have mentioned a couple years ago.

YEAR	TEAM	LVL	AGE	PA	DRC+	BABIP	BRR	FRAA	WARP
2018	NOR	AAA	24	490	105	.278	4.7	RF(88): -14.1, LF(24): 1.9, CF(3): -0.6	-0.2
2018	BAL	MLB	24	47	88	.269	0.5	LF(9): 4.4, RF(6): -0.4	0.5
2019	NOR	AAA	25	277	130	.324	-2.1	LF(30): -1.2, RF(22): 1.6	1.4
2019	BAL	MLB	25	142	83	.268	-0.3	RF(26): -1.8, LF(11): -0.5	-0.2
2020	BAL	MLB	26	112	100	.233	-0.3	RF(21): 3.5, LF(10): 0.1	0.7
2021 FS	BAL	MLB	27	600	95	.275	0.0	LF 2, RF 0	1.2
2021 DC	BAL	MLB	27	333	95	.275	0.0	LF 1, RF 0	0.7

Terrin Vavra SS

Born: 05/12/97   Age: 24   Bats: L   Throws: R
Height: 6'1"   Weight: 185   Origin: Round 3, 2018 Draft (#96 overall)

YEAR	TEAM	LVL	AGE	PA	R	2B	3B	HR	RBI	BB	K	SB	CS	AVG/OBP/SLG
2018	BOI	SS	21	199	22	8	4	4	26	26	40	9	1	.302/.396/.467
2019	ASH	LO-A	22	453	79	32	1	10	52	62	62	18	9	.318/.409/.489
2021 FS	BAL	MLB	24	600	53	24	3	11	57	42	151	10	5	.230/.288/.349

Comparables: Cole Figueroa, Jurickson Profar, Chase d'Arnaud

Part of the Mychal Givens deal. He's got an outstanding name, the ability to play both middle infield spots and some legit offensive potential. If he proves he can hit for some power outside of Colorado's minor-league launching pads, he'll earn a bigger blurb in next year's book.

YEAR	TEAM	LVL	AGE	PA	DRC+	BABIP	BRR	FRAA	WARP
2018	BOI	SS	21	199	142	.373	-0.5	SS(28): 0.8, 2B(16): -2.0	0.7
2019	ASH	LO-A	22	453	151	.350	0.4	SS(53): -1.4, 2B(41): 2.7	4.0
2021 FS	BAL	MLB	24	600	75	.297	0.7	SS 0, 2B 2	0.2

Michael Baumann RHP

Born: 09/10/95   Age: 25   Bats: R   Throws: R
Height: 6'4"   Weight: 225   Origin: Round 3, 2017 Draft (#98 overall)

YEAR	TEAM	LVL	AGE	W	L	SV	G	GS	IP	H	HR	BB/9	K/9	K	GB%	BABIP
2018	DEL	LO-A	22	5	0	0	7	7	38	23	0	3.1	11.1	47	50.6%	.284
2018	FRE	HI-A	22	8	5	0	17	17	92²	82	9	3.9	5.7	59	32.9%	.263
2019	FRE	HI-A	23	1	4	0	11	11	54	40	2	4.0	12.8	77	43.1%	.317
2019	BOW	AA	23	6	2	1	13	11	70	45	2	2.7	8.4	65	41.4%	.242
2021 FS	BAL	MLB	25	9	8	0	26	26	150	132	21	5.0	8.8	146	40.3%	.277
2021 DC	BAL	MLB	25	2	2	0	9	9	40.7	35	5	5.0	8.8	39	40.3%	.277

Comparables: Ryan Borucki, Patrick Murphy, Matt Hall

An average fastball with a few average secondary offerings, a track record of high-minors success, a decent chance to stick at the back of the rotation and the same name as the dude who writes good stuff for The Ringer. What else do you need to know? He's now on the 40-man roster, so he'll definitely be up and pitching in the coming season. He's in a group of nauseous toddlers (young hurlers) alongside Kyle Bradish, Keegan Akin, Dean Kremer and Kevin Smith who will all get chances to start in 2021 and will all have to impress to remain starters long term. One last irrelevant thing: the Wikipedia page for Baumann's high school, Mahtomedi Senior High in Minnesota, does not have a notable alumni section. If he'd attended an average high school with a few half-famous alumni scattered around, an 18th-century congressman here and a highly respected concert cellist there, he'd probably already be worthy of inclusion. But no, according to the internet masses, neither Baumann nor any of his fellow Mahtomedi Zephyr compatriots are worthy of that title yet. It will be interesting to see just how good Baumann has to be to break that barrier, or whether his impending big-league debut will be enough to rewrite history on its own.

YEAR	TEAM	LVL	AGE	WHIP	ERA	DRA-	WARP	MPH	FB%	WHF	CSP
2018	DEL	LO-A	22	0.95	1.42	68	0.9				
2018	FRE	HI-A	22	1.32	3.88	171	-2.9				
2019	FRE	HI-A	23	1.19	3.83	77	0.8				
2019	BOW	AA	23	0.94	2.31	57	1.8				
2021 FS	BAL	MLB	25	1.43	4.42	97	1.7				
2021 DC	BAL	MLB	25	1.43	4.42	97	0.5				

Kyle Bradish RHP

Born: 09/12/96   Age: 24   Bats: R   Throws: R
Height: 6'4"   Weight: 190   Origin: Round 4, 2018 Draft (#121 overall)

YEAR	TEAM	LVL	AGE	W	L	SV	G	GS	IP	H	HR	BB/9	K/9	K	GB%	BABIP
2019	IE	HI-A	22	6	7	0	24	18	101	90	9	4.7	10.7	120	43.9%	.314
2021 FS	BAL	MLB	24	2	3	0	57	0	50	45	8	5.9	8.7	48	41.2%	.279

Comparables: Pierce Johnson, Dietrich Enns, Albert Abreu

Dylan Bundy's leaving Baltimore and immediately fulfilling his potential as a top-10 pitcher in the American League was a tough pill for the Birds to swallow, but Bradish might be the spoonful of sugar that helps the medicine go down. He was the breakout superstar of the Orioles' alternate site in Bowie, sporting a mid-90s heatball and two average secondaries, all from a deceptive motion. He's not as experienced or proven in the high minors as Akin and Kremer and the ceiling isn't as high as Hall or Rodriguez, but if the 24-year-old replicates his 2020 scrimmage performance, he has a shot to break into the major-league rotation in 2021 and turn some heads.

YEAR	TEAM	LVL	AGE	WHIP	ERA	DRA-	WARP	MPH	FB%	WHF	CSP
2019	IE	HI-A	22	1.42	4.28	99	0.1				
2021 FS	BAL	MLB	24	1.57	5.20	115	-0.2				

Aaron Brooks   RHP

Born: 04/27/90   Age: 31   Bats: R   Throws: R
Height: 6'4"   Weight: 230   Origin: Round 9, 2011 Draft (#276 overall)

YEAR	TEAM	LVL	AGE	W	L	SV	G	GS	IP	H	HR	BB/9	K/9	K	GB%	BABIP
2018	RMV	AAA	28	9	4	0	26	15	99^1	100	8	2.5	6.7	74	54.9%	.309
2018	OAK	MLB	28	0	0	0	3	0	2^2	1	0	6.8	3.4	1	71.4%	.143
2019	BAL	MLB	29	4	5	0	14	12	59^2	69	9	3.0	5.9	39	45.5%	.312
2019	OAK	MLB	29	2	3	0	15	6	50^1	49	12	2.5	7.7	43	40.3%	.261
2020	KIA	KBO	30	11	4	0	23	23	151^1	131	4	1.0	7.7	130		
2021 FS	BAL	MLB	31	2	2	0	57	0	50	51	8	2.7	7.1	39	44.6%	.287

Comparables: Chris Stratton, Jordan Lyles, Mike Wright

For four and a half months, Brooks was one of the best pitchers in the KBO. He had the league's top FIP and lowest home run rate, and was one of the main drivers behind a surprisingly decent Kia Tigers club as they battled for the playoffs. Then, real life intervened. Back home in Kansas, Brooks' wife and two children were involved in a serious car accident. Everyone survived, but two-year-old Westin was badly hurt and ultimately lost an eye; Brooks immediately flew back to the United States to be with his family. His departure effectively ended Brooks's season and with it any real chance Kia had of reaching the playoffs. In the wake of that disappointment, the ensuing support of the Brooks family from the Tigers, their fans, and the rest of the league speaks volumes about the Korean League's generosity of spirit and order of priorities. Everyone on the Tigers, and many other players from around the league, wrote Westin's initials on their caps. Kia started a "praying for the Brooks family" campaign and hung Aaron's jersey in the dugout for the remainder of the season. A continent away, the Brooks family regularly expressed the gratitude they felt toward the community in Gwangju. In lieu of testing big-league waters after a very successful season, Aaron immediately re-signed with the Tigers. In a year where baseball often seemed less important than ever, this was perhaps the finest example of the game's capacity to unify and uplift.

YEAR	TEAM	LVL	AGE	WHIP	ERA	DRA-	WARP	MPH	FB%	WHF	CSP
2018	RMV	AAA	28	1.29	3.35	98	1.0				
2018	OAK	MLB	28	1.12	0.00	105	0.0	94.1	45.2%	0.0%	
2019	BAL	MLB	29	1.49	6.18	120	-0.1	93.7	50.3%	18.6%	
2019	OAK	MLB	29	1.25	5.01	130	-0.4	94.3	58.4%	20.8%	
2020	KIA	KBO	30	1.02	2.50						
2021 FS	BAL	MLB	31	1.33	4.61	103	0.2	94.0	53.8%	19.3%	47.8%

DL Hall LHP

Born: 09/19/98   Age: 22   Bats: L   Throws: L
Height: 6'2"   Weight: 195   Origin: Round 1, 2017 Draft (#21 overall)

YEAR	TEAM	LVL	AGE	W	L	SV	G	GS	IP	H	HR	BB/9	K/9	K	GB%	BABIP
2018	DEL	LO-A	19	2	7	0	22	20	94¹	68	6	4.0	9.5	100	41.6%	.268
2019	FRE	HI-A	20	4	5	1	19	17	80²	53	3	6.0	12.9	116	34.1%	.301
2021 FS	BAL	MLB	22	2	3	0	57	0	50	45	8	7.1	10.1	56	38.1%	.293
2021 DC	BAL	MLB	22	0	1	0	3	3	14.7	13	2	7.1	10.1	16	38.1%	.293

Comparables: Brailyn Marquez, Dustin May, Alex Reyes

You know what doesn't grow on trees? Pineapples. Oh, also lefty pitching prospects with fastballs in the mid-to-high 90s and two above-average secondary pitches like Hall. His stuff is up there with anyone in the minors, and his strikeout numbers in High-A in 2019 reflected that. He brought that nasty stuff to the alternate site in 2020 and threw pretty well against the stiffest competition that the 22-year-old had ever faced. The other thing you need to know about Hall: He also walks a lot of hitters (check that 2019 line again). There's a world where he figures out the command/control part without sacrificing the zippiness of the arsenal, turning into a strikeout monster atop the Orioles rotation for a half-decade. There's also a world where the walks stick around forever and he's a more fun version of Robbie Ray. There's also a world where we're all just upside down clones of ourselves wearing pink pajamas and baseball doesn't exist, never did and never will. There's endless realities y'all. In most of them, DL Hall spends 2021 in Double-A before debuting in 2022.

YEAR	TEAM	LVL	AGE	WHIP	ERA	DRA-	WARP	MPH	FB%	WHF	CSP
2018	DEL	LO-A	19	1.17	2.10	78	1.6				
2019	FRE	HI-A	20	1.33	3.46	76	1.3				
2021 FS	BAL	MLB	22	1.70	5.90	122	-0.4				
2021 DC	BAL	MLB	22	1.70	5.90	122	0.0				

Félix Hernández   RHP

Born: 04/08/86   Age: 35   Bats: R   Throws: R
Height: 6'3"   Weight: 208   Origin: International Free Agent, 2002

YEAR	TEAM	LVL	AGE	W	L	SV	G	GS	IP	H	HR	BB/9	K/9	K	GB%	BABIP
2018	SEA	MLB	32	8	14	0	29	28	155²	159	27	3.4	7.2	125	46.5%	.288
2019	SEA	MLB	33	1	8	0	15	15	71²	85	17	3.1	7.2	57	48.5%	.311
2021 FS	BAL	MLB	35	2	2	0	57	0	50	48	7	3.3	7.9	44	47.3%	.287

Comparables: Jake Peavy, Josh Beckett, Cole Hamels

We never got a chance to see what Hernández was capable of in his first season outside of Seattle, as the former Cy Young winner opted out of the season owing to COVID-19 concerns. That's probably for the best: The thought of him in a non-Mariners uniform is genuinely upsetting.

YEAR	TEAM	LVL	AGE	WHIP	ERA	DRA-	WARP	MPH	FB%	WHF	CSP
2018	SEA	MLB	32	1.40	5.55	118	0.0	91.1	43.3%	19.8%	
2019	SEA	MLB	33	1.53	6.40	145	-1.0	91.4	39.5%	21.8%	
2021 FS	BAL	MLB	35	1.34	4.28	102	0.2	91.2	41.4%	20.8%	47.4%

Wade LeBlanc   LHP

Born: 08/07/84   Age: 36   Bats: L   Throws: L
Height: 6'3"   Weight: 215   Origin: Round 2, 2006 Draft (#61 overall)

YEAR	TEAM	LVL	AGE	W	L	SV	G	GS	IP	H	HR	BB/9	K/9	K	GB%	BABIP
2018	SEA	MLB	33	9	5	0	32	27	162	151	24	2.2	7.2	130	36.4%	.274
2019	SEA	MLB	34	6	7	0	26	8	121¹	145	28	2.3	6.8	92	40.2%	.309
2020	BAL	MLB	35	1	0	0	6	6	22¹	27	6	3.2	5.2	13	37.0%	.280
2021 FS	BAL	MLB	36	2	3	0	57	0	50	53	10	2.6	6.5	36	38.6%	.287

Comparables: Zach Duke, Edwin Jackson, Ian Kennedy

It was obvious that the Orioles rotation wouldn't be winning any ERA titles the moment they snatched up Tommy Milone and LeBlanc—not one, but two rejects from a 2019 Mariners rotation that finished tied for fourth to last in the league in DRA. LeBlanc made six starts for Baltimore. The first one was alright, the second one was good, the next three were stanky and then he left the final one with a "stress reaction in his throwing elbow." He's a free agent as this book goes to press, and while the market for 36-year-old lefties averaging 87 on the fastball won't be scorching this year, there's no way we've seen the last of LeBlanc. Nine lives on this one.

YEAR	TEAM	LVL	AGE	WHIP	ERA	DRA-	WARP	MPH	FB%	WHF	CSP
2018	SEA	MLB	33	1.18	3.72	113	0.4	87.5	61.1%	21.9%	
2019	SEA	MLB	34	1.45	5.71	164	-3.4	87.3	58.2%	22.2%	
2020	BAL	MLB	35	1.57	8.06	158	-0.5	88.2	52.2%	25.0%	
2021 FS	BAL	MLB	36	1.36	4.91	108	0.0	87.5	58.2%	22.5%	47.8%

Zac Lowther LHP

Born: 04/30/96   Age: 25   Bats: L   Throws: L
Height: 6'2"   Weight: 235   Origin: Round 2, 2017 Draft (#74 overall)

YEAR	TEAM	LVL	AGE	W	L	SV	G	GS	IP	H	HR	BB/9	K/9	K	GB%	BABIP
2018	DEL	LO-A	22	3	1	0	6	6	31	12	2	2.6	14.8	51	33.3%	.192
2018	FRE	HI-A	22	5	3	0	17	16	92²	74	6	2.5	9.7	100	36.8%	.292
2019	BOW	AA	23	13	7	0	26	26	148	102	8	3.8	9.4	154	39.4%	.260
2021 FS	BAL	MLB	25	2	2	0	57	0	50	44	7	4.1	9.4	52	38.8%	.284
2021 DC	BAL	MLB	25	2	2	0	6	9	39.7	35	5	4.1	9.4	41	38.8%	.284

Comparables: David Peterson, Brendan McKay, Tucker Davidson

One of the Orioles' many low-90s-fastball-toting, left-handed, back-end-rotation hopefuls. The stuff isn't particularly sexy, but he has always posted gaudy strikeout numbers, dating back to his days at Xavier.

YEAR	TEAM	LVL	AGE	WHIP	ERA	DRA-	WARP	MPH	FB%	WHF	CSP
2018	DEL	LO-A	22	0.68	1.16	49	1.0				
2018	FRE	HI-A	22	1.08	2.53	82	1.6				
2019	BOW	AA	23	1.11	2.55	85	1.4				
2021 FS	BAL	MLB	25	1.34	4.14	93	0.4				
2021 DC	BAL	MLB	25	1.34	4.14	93	0.5				

Grayson Rodriguez   RHP

Born: 11/16/99   Age: 21   Bats: L   Throws: R
Height: 6'5"   Weight: 220   Origin: Round 1, 2018 Draft (#11 overall)

YEAR	TEAM	LVL	AGE	W	L	SV	G	GS	IP	H	HR	BB/9	K/9	K	GB%	BABIP
2018	ORI	ROK	18	0	2	0	9	8	19¹	17	0	3.3	9.3	20	43.4%	.321
2019	DEL	LO-A	19	10	4	0	20	20	94	57	4	3.4	12.4	129	44.2%	.262
2021 FS	BAL	MLB	21	2	2	0	57	0	50	43	7	5.1	9.4	52	39.2%	.279

Comparables: Hunter Harvey, Tyler Glasnow, Danny Duffy

Over the last decade-plus, Baltimore (or more specifically Bowie, Frederick and Delmarva) has been an abyss where high-pick pitching prospects go to underperform or wallow in obscurity. Even the arms that reached Camden Yards—the Arrietas, the Bundys, the Gausmans—never fully put it together in Baltimore, only to succeed elsewhere. All that is to say: Rodriguez is the first test of the new Orioles regime's ability to develop pitching, because boy oh boy does this dude have the talent to succeed. He's a hulking tree of a man, armed with all the characteristics you want in a future frontline starter: a mid- to high-90s fastball, a plus slider and feel for what could one day be a plus changeup. He's smart, he's pitcher-mean, he knows he's gonna be good and, so far, everything is going to plan. Rodriguez almost certainly won't be up in 2021. However, there's a small but real chance he's the number one pitching prospect in baseball this time next year.

YEAR	TEAM	LVL	AGE	WHIP	ERA	DRA-	WARP	MPH	FB%	WHF	CSP
2018	ORI	ROK	18	1.24	1.40						
2019	DEL	LO-A	19	0.99	2.68	55	2.8				
2021 FS	BAL	MLB	21	1.44	4.61	104	0.1				

Kevin Smith   LHP

Born: 05/13/97   Age: 24   Bats: R   Throws: L
Height: 6'5"   Weight: 200   Origin: Round 7, 2018 Draft (#200 overall)

YEAR	TEAM	LVL	AGE	W	L	SV	G	GS	IP	H	HR	BB/9	K/9	K	GB%	BABIP
2018	BRK	SS	21	4	1	0	12	3	23²	12	1	2.3	10.6	28	49.0%	.220
2019	STL	HI-A	22	5	5	0	17	17	85²	83	5	2.5	10.7	102	44.1%	.359
2019	BNG	AA	22	3	2	0	6	6	31¹	25	1	4.3	8.0	28	39.3%	.289
2021 FS	BAL	MLB	24	2	3	0	57	0	50	47	8	4.3	8.7	48	39.2%	.287

Comparables: David Peterson, Bernardo Flores Jr., Mitch Keller

See: Lowther, Zac, except he's from Georgia, came to Baltimore in the Miguel Castro trade and has a league-average slider. If you're interested in this type of profile, buckle up because there are two more O's like this.

YEAR	TEAM	LVL	AGE	WHIP	ERA	DRA-	WARP	MPH	FB%	WHF	CSP
2018	BRK	SS	21	0.76	0.76	130	-0.3				
2019	STL	HI-A	22	1.25	3.05	88	0.7				
2019	BNG	AA	22	1.28	3.45	115	-0.2				
2021 FS	BAL	MLB	24	1.42	4.71	106	0.1				

Alexander Wells   LHP

Born: 02/27/97   Age: 24   Bats: L   Throws: L
Height: 6'1"   Weight: 190   Origin: International Free Agent, 2015

YEAR	TEAM	LVL	AGE	W	L	SV	G	GS	IP	H	HR	BB/9	K/9	K	GB%	BABIP
2018	FRE	HI-A	21	7	8	0	24	24	135	142	19	2.2	6.7	101	35.3%	.302
2019	BOW	AA	22	8	6	0	24	24	137¹	123	10	1.6	6.9	105	40.8%	.276
2021 FS	BAL	MLB	24	2	2	0	57	0	50	51	9	2.2	6.5	36	40.2%	.280
2021 DC	BAL	MLB	24	3	2	0	22	6	40	41	7	2.2	6.5	29	40.2%	.280

Comparables: Brock Burke, JoJo Romero, Gabriel Ynoa

See: Lowther, Zac and Smith, Kevin, but Australian, a slower fastball, less impressive strikeout numbers and he wears cool goggles on the mound.

YEAR	TEAM	LVL	AGE	WHIP	ERA	DRA-	WARP	MPH	FB%	WHF	CSP
2018	FRE	HI-A	21	1.30	3.47	95	1.4				
2019	BOW	AA	22	1.07	2.95	93	0.7				
2021 FS	BAL	MLB	24	1.27	4.36	100	0.2				
2021 DC	BAL	MLB	24	1.27	4.36	100	0.3				

Bruce Zimmermann   LHP

Born: 02/09/95   Age: 26   Bats: L   Throws: L
Height: 6'2"   Weight: 215   Origin: Round 5, 2017 Draft (#140 overall)

YEAR	TEAM	LVL	AGE	W	L	SV	G	GS	IP	H	HR	BB/9	K/9	K	GB%	BABIP
2018	ROM	LO-A	23	7	3	0	14	14	84²	74	5	1.9	10.5	99	46.6%	.322
2018	BOW	AA	23	2	3	0	5	5	21¹	25	2	3.0	6.8	16	27.4%	.329
2018	MIS	AA	23	2	1	0	6	6	28²	25	3	6.0	8.2	26	37.5%	.293
2019	BOW	AA	24	5	3	0	18	17	101¹	88	9	3.0	9.0	101	39.6%	.283
2019	NOR	AAA	24	2	3	0	7	7	38²	44	3	4.2	7.7	33	44.7%	.345
2020	BAL	MLB	25	0	0	0	2	1	7	6	2	2.6	9.0	7	50.0%	.222
2021 FS	BAL	MLB	26	9	9	0	26	26	150	150	26	3.6	8.1	134	40.7%	.292
2021 DC	BAL	MLB	26	7	8	0	45	22	97.3	97	17	3.6	8.1	87	40.7%	.292

Comparables: Anthony Misiewicz, Max Fried, Framber Valdez

See: Lowther, Zac; Smith, Kevin and Wells, Alex, except Zimmermann is actually from Baltimore, so he'll be in the newspaper a bunch and he's probably a smidge less likely to stick in the back of a rotation. Got rocked in a 2020 cup of coffee.

Baltimore Orioles 2021

YEAR	TEAM	LVL	AGE	WHIP	ERA	DRA-	WARP	MPH	FB%	WHF	CSP
2018	ROM	LO-A	23	1.09	2.76	64	2.1				
2018	BOW	AA	23	1.50	5.06	153	-0.5				
2018	MIS	AA	23	1.53	3.14	105	0.1				
2019	BOW	AA	24	1.20	2.58	90	0.7				
2019	NOR	AAA	24	1.60	4.89	117	0.4				
2020	BAL	MLB	25	1.14	7.71	106	0.0	93.7	51.4%	19.2%	
2021 FS	BAL	MLB	26	1.40	4.85	105	1.0	93.7	51.4%	19.2%	52.1%
2021 DC	BAL	MLB	26	1.40	4.85	105	0.5	93.7	51.4%	19.2%	52.1%

Orioles Prospects

The State of the System:

The Orioles 2020 draft strategy didn't seem to quite come off, but it remains a deep system albeit lacking in high upside profiles. Also, Ryan Mountcastle is still here somehow.

The Top Ten:

──────── ★ ★ ★ *2021 Top 101 Prospect* **#2** ★ ★ ★ ────────

1
Adley Rutschman   C   OFP: 70   ETA: Mid-to-late 2021
Born: 02/06/98   Age: 23   Bats: S   Throws: R   Height: 6'2"   Weight: 220
Origin: Round 1, 2019 Draft (#1 overall)

The Report: One of the best catching prospects in recent memory. Rutschman is a switch-hitter with a quick swing from both sides of the plate. His swing plane is made for the modern game. He controls the barrel. His plate approach is solid. His power is at least plus and we think he'll get it into games. He's an average runner, which is superb for a catcher. He projects as an above-average to excellent defender in all facets, including pitch framing. He has the potential to be a top-of-the-line two-way catcher with few weaknesses.

Development Track: Rutschman was brought to the alternate site midway through summer camp, essentially eliminating any chance he'd have to force his way onto the major-league roster. We suspect given their backgrounds that the new Orioles regime is going to be extremely aggressive with service time manipulation, so we aren't holding that against him developmentally. Everything is still on track here, and Rutschman remains one of the best prospects in the game.

Variance: Low. There's always going to be a certain amount of variance attached with the catching position, but we think there's an unusually high likelihood that he'll be at least a first-division starter.

Mark Barry's Fantasy Take: I'll be honest, I kinda thought Ben Carsley's love/hate/loathe relationship to catching prospects was a bit. But after writing fantasy analysis for said catching prospects for a little while now, I'm starting to wonder if our pal doesn't have a point. Catching prospect fatigue is REAL.

All that said, Rutschman is about as good a bet as any to be a successful fantasy contributor behind the dish. He can hit, hit for power, and he's so good defensively, there's no doubt he's staying behind the plate. He's one of the five or 10 best prospects in the game, and while I'd personally bump him down a few spots for the "catcher penalty" it's pretty much Rutschman and everyone else as far as fantasy catching prospects are concerned.

───── ★ ★ ★ *2021 Top 101 Prospect* **#28** ★ ★ ★ ─────

2

Ryan Mountcastle   1B   OFP: 60   ETA: Debuted in 2020
Born: 02/18/97   Age: 24   Bats: R   Throws: R   Height: 6'3"   Weight: 210
Origin: Round 1, 2015 Draft (#36 overall)

The Report: Mountcastle was a consistent offensive force at the plate throughout his minor league career. He hit between .276 and .314 at all his full-season spots, turned doubles power into 20+ home run power as he filled out, and always did enough damage on contact to prop up an approach that even the most genteel and restrained among us would describe as "aggressive." There's always the risk that this type of slugger will get exposed against major-league pitching. Mountcastle's bat speed is above-average but not special, and there's some stomp and lift in the swing, some holes you might be able to exploit. As he's filled out and added that home run pop, he's also slid down the defensive spectrum and was handed a first base glove at the beginning of 2019 after being drafted as a shortstop four years earlier.

Development Track: Honestly, the fact that Mountcastle is still eligible for this list at all—by a mere four at-bats—is a testament to service time manipulation. His major-league debut was an unqualified success. He posted league-average-ish strikeout and walk rates, and if he can do that going forward ... well he won't hit .330, but a perennial .300 hitter might be in play. That's unlikely to continue, though, as the underlying zone control and contact rates don't support it, nor does the minor league track record. All together, Mountcastle looks more or less like we expected, plus 50 points of batting average or so, which can happen in a quarter of a season. We're more confident he's a good major-league hitter now, but good remains .280 with 25 home runs and plenty of doubles. Maybe a few extra walks now, to boot. He did look perfectly serviceable in left field, despite only having playing there for 26 games in the minors. Mountcastle played some first base as well and don't be shocked to see him DH now and again. He's broadly fine wherever he stands, but it all looks a lot better when he's standing in the batter's box.

Variance: Low. There's enough of a chance there've been some real approach gains here that Mountcastle can get to a plus regular despite very limited defensive value and the absence of the kind of plus-plus pop you associate with your Role 6 corner mashers. He feels more like a safe 55 type. Maybe one season that looks better when he has a nice 150-game run of BABIP fortune. And then maybe one season that gets non-tendered after he hits .250 with a few too many Ks (and then goes to the Rays and rips off three more solid seasons, as long as we are reading the auguries).

Mark Barry's Fantasy Take: Look, it's going to be awfully hard for Mountcastle to maintain his pretty good strikeout rate (and in turn, batting average) with a swinging-strike rate five percentage points higher than league average. But despite (or maybe because of?) his uber-aggressiveness, Mountcastle was impressive in his debut. I would be remiss if I didn't drop a Nick Castellanos comp in this space for the third consecutive season because it still feels so right. I'd have Mountcastle among the top-30ish dynasty prospects in the game.

──────── ★ ★ ★ *2021 Top 101 Prospect* **#30** ★ ★ ★ ────────

3 **Grayson Rodriguez RHP** OFP: 60 ETA: 2022
Born: 11/16/99 Age: 21 Bats: L Throws: R Height: 6'5" Weight: 220
Origin: Round 1, 2018 Draft (#11 overall)

The Report: I got three Rodriguez looks in the second half of 2019. Not only was he progressing compared to early-season looks from other BP prospect staff, he also progressed from when I saw him in early-July to when I saw him in late-August. By the end of the season, he was consistently sitting 94-97 and touching 98, up from sitting 91-93 and touching 95 in Ben Spanier's April look. He's flashed both a plus slider and a plus changeup projection for us, along with a curveball that has a nice shape but tends to run together with the slider in the slurviness, as well as an occasional cutter. There's a lot of potential here, some of it already actualized, and a pretty good shot to stay in the rotation all the way up to the majors.

Development Track: Like Rutschman, Rodriguez wasn't brought to summer camp initially; he was added to the alternate site roster around the time the major-league team broke camp. His alternate site velocity was essentially identical to our late-summer 2019 looks, so he held the fastball gains, if not quite to a full season then at least to the next year. We probably need to see it over 100 innings to go truly hog wild with his projection, but he's on the cusp of the top pitching prospects in the game.

Variance: Medium. It's mostly all the generic good young pitcher risk, but if you want to start nitpicking he could use better separation of his offerings on the curve/slider/cutter continuum.

Mark Barry's Fantasy Take: I don't mean this to sound too hot take-y, but I'm not sure there are five pitching prospects I'd take over Rodriguez, and if there were, he'd surely be in the top six or seven. I love the fact that he brought his high-90s fastball velocity back with him to the alternative site, giving him three potentially plus pitches in his arsenal. It almost doesn't matter if the curveball ever fully gets there. Even better? You might not have to pay top-five prices to scoop him up.

───── ★ ★ ★ *2021 Top 101 Prospect* **#53** ★ ★ ★ ─────

4

DL Hall   LHP   OFP: 60   ETA: 2022
Born: 09/19/98   Age: 22   Bats: L   Throws: L   Height: 6'2"   Weight: 195
Origin: Round 1, 2017 Draft (#21 overall)

The Report: The alternate site was good to Hall. The young lefty took full advantage of the opportunity to battle against higher-level hitters, and managed to upgrade his game all around. His fastball remains his top offering, regularly sitting 95-98 and flirting with 99. Exploding with late life, the added velocity only makes it more dangerous. Between the fastball and his two above-average secondaries—a curve with serious sharp bite and a vastly improved changeup—Hall's built up a solid arsenal. He isn't afraid to attack hitters. He's got impact stuff and he knows it. The potential here is obvious, and there's a reason Hall's been high on this list year after year, and he only continues to progress.

Development Track: Hall's high walk rate was his biggest hurdle coming into the season, a struggle to reliably master both control and command overshadowing his strikeout numbers. When he can find the zone, he can easily elicit big swings and misses, as well as weak contact, but it's the inability to find the zone that's been the problem. He's made great strides on the control front, and will likely spend the majority of the 2021 season refining his command. The ceiling is still high here.

Variance: Medium. There's been substantial improvement in his control, but he still hasn't fully developed his command quite yet. Consistency is key, and Hall's consistently shown reliever risk.

Mark Barry's Fantasy Take: Not to beat a dead horse (which btw I totally wouldn't recommend anyway, it just seems cruel), but I would've loved to see Hall pitch in 2020. The stuff is undeniable, and reports of increased velocity from the left side are tantalizing. But we mostly knew this last year, and still have the same concerns about ALL OF THOSE WALKS. Hall is still a top-100 name for me, but until we know that he's scaled back on the free passes, he's a pretty big relief risk.

───── ★ ★ ★ *2021 Top 101 Prospect* **#66** ★ ★ ★ ─────

5

Heston Kjerstad   OF   OFP: 60   ETA: Early 2023 (under current CBA rules)
Born: 02/12/99   Age: 22   Bats: L   Throws: R   Height: 6'3"   Weight: 220
Origin: Round 1, 2020 Draft (#2 overall)

The Report: We were all told to expect the unexpected when it came to this year's June draft, and the warnings proved true almost immediately as the Orioles popped Kjerstad second overall on an under-slot deal as they saw him among the best college hitters in the class. And indeed, he is. While sliding in at No. 7 on our pre-draft rankings, it wasn't that much a stretch to see him picked so high. The bat control and power shown in two-plus years at Arkansas were evident. Even with a slightly unorthodox stroke he is able to make contact in every quadrant in the zone with hands that can adjust to velocity mid-pitch. This ability is both a gift and a curse, as he tends to swing at a lot of pitches outside the zone, too.

Development Track: There is room for added mass on his 6-foot-3 frame, and maybe not the good kind, either. Keeping his body lean so he can stay in a corner outfield spot while maintaining at least average speed on the basepaths will help get his bat in the lineup sooner rather than later. He has dabbled at first base in the past, but there is far more value in his profile as an outfielder. Who knows if the O's will bother to attempt to refine his pitch selection; the kid has raked for nearly three years in the best college conference, needing refinement in other areas of his game instead of nit-picking his strengths.

Variance: Medium. Depending on which way the body goes the OFP could go a full grade up or down. The bat is likely to play regardless.

Mark Barry's Fantasy Take: Looking back, I was probably a little unfair to Kjerstad on draft day. Sure, the aggressive approach could require an overhaul against advanced pitching, but complaining about a 20ish percent strikeout rate and a walk rate under eight percent when you're hitting .340 and slugging nearly .600 in your college career is a little like being miffed that the $100 bill you found on the street wasn't also wrapped in $100 bills. There are still other bats from the 2020 draft I'd prefer, but Kjerstad is a top-60 guy for fantasy with the possibility of solid contributions in four categories.

6 **Dean Kremer** **RHP** OFP: 50 ETA: Debuted in 2020
Born: 01/07/96 Age: 25 Bats: R Throws: R Height: 6'3" Weight: 185
Origin: Round 14, 2016 Draft (#431 overall)

The Report: Kremer was effective throughout his minor league career, consistently posting hefty strikeout numbers. We had him slated to debut this year, and he had all the stuff to back it up, so it was only a matter of time before he broke out of the alternate site and made his way to Baltimore. Three of his four starts were clear successes, with one unfortunate outing that ballooned his ERA to 4.82 for the season. Rough appearance aside, Kremer gave the O's a great look at what he can do. He threw his 92-94 fastball half of the time, as expected, and the offering topped out at 96. Paired with his equally impressive mid-70s curveball with serious drop, Kremer held his steady strikeout numbers, striking out 22 in 18 2/3 innings. He has the ability to pitch fairly deep into games by today's standards, only being pulled before completing five innings once.

Development Track: His fastball and curve remain high quality, above-average pitches, but the rest of his stuff lingers between barely average and just good enough. The slider is a self-proclaimed work in progress; there's not much break and while he can get it over for strikes, it's inconsistent. His mid-80s changeup exists, although sightings are rare. It's hard to gauge its true effectiveness, as he threw it fewer than a dozen times this season. He's still ramping up to a four-pitch mix; refining his third and fourth offerings would make him a potential middle-of-the-rotation guy. Kremer may slide back into a relief role at some point, but he's definitely solidified his role as a starter thus far.

Variance: Low. Kremer's proven he can handle the big stage.

Mark Barry's Fantasy Take: Do you ever comb through stat lines to find relatively unheralded prospects with fairly decent numbers, plant your flag early in their career, and then become unreasonably attached to them, inflating their value in your head and in your head only? That's me with Kremer. Nice guy. Probably an SP5/streamer, though.

7 **Ryan McKenna   CF**   OFP: 50   ETA: 2021
Born: 02/14/97   Age: 24   Bats: R   Throws: R   Height: 5'11"   Weight: 185
Origin: Round 4, 2015 Draft (#133 overall)

The Report: You would never call McKenna a five-tool outfielder in the way we use that term as prospect writers, but you can put at least a 5 at every spot on the scouting sheet—well, maybe not his arm unless you want to give his below-average arm strength a bump for accuracy. The problem is you have to squint a little to get any of those 5s to 55s. He is a good enough defender in center, but above-average might be a stretch. His approach can make the hit tool play more to average The power is more average raw than average game at present. It all adds up to a major leaguer, and one who could end up greater than the sum of his tools, but one with little room to fall short and still carry a starter's profile.

Development Track: I expected McKenna to perhaps get a look at some point in 2020, but the Orioles outfield was actually pretty good, especially after Mountcastle took over left field. You could note that the bat hasn't really been amazing in the upper minors and he didn't force the issue at the alternate site. Really, nothing much has changed for McKenna, other than perhaps a tougher road to playing time if you believe in the Anthony Santander breakout.

Variance: Medium. The broad base of skills on both offense and defense should keep McKenna employed as a bench outfielder for most of his team control years even if the bat doesn't play enough to make him a starter.

Mark Barry's Fantasy Take: Like Jeffrey said, the Orioles' outfield was actually fairly decent this season. That said, it's also probably not a great sign that you couldn't wrestle away reps from anyone in the Orioles' outfield. McKenna hasn't really been an impact bat since his 2018 stint in High-A, so bench outfielder sounds right—which means you can probably pass unless your league carries 350 or so prospects.

8 **Kyle Bradish   RHP**   OFP: 50   ETA: Mid-to-Late 2021
Born: 09/12/96   Age: 24   Bats: R   Throws: R   Height: 6'4"   Weight: 190
Origin: Round 4, 2018 Draft (#121 overall)

The Report: The standout from the Dylan Bundy trade, Bradish turned the most heads at the alternate site, showing off a 3-4 mph uptick in velocity. His fastball, one of his strongest offerings, now sits in the mid 90s, touching as high as 97. He boasts a four-pitch mix, including a high quality top-spinning curveball and a high-80s slider; both effective put away pitches. His firm changeup isn't as polished as his other pitches, but it plays up because of his heater, and he has enough feel to pump it through the zone. Bradish's deceptive delivery serves him well, throwing off batters and keeping them unbalanced. The 6-foot-4 righty uses every inch of his large frame to his advantage.

Development Track: Previous issues with command of his secondaries aren't nearly as prominent as they once were, although there's always room for improvement there. He's aggressive on the mound, a more efficient delivery granting confidence and more pitches in the strike zone. The stuff is powerful, easily above average, and his fastball regularly flashes plus. The changeup is still only decent, but alongside the rest of his arsenal it's a solid weapon and he's learning how to utilize it. With no real experience at higher levels, the Orioles may be cautious with him, but I fully expect Bradish to make a case for himself and find a way to crack the starting rotation before the season ends, or appear in the bullpen, at the very least.

Variance: Low. Aside from the pitchers who have already made their debuts, Bradish is the closest to being major league ready. The stuff is great and he's incredibly poised; the opportunities from the big club will come sooner rather than later.

Mark Barry's Fantasy Take: Righty destined for middle relief adds four ticks to his fastball and all of his other pitches now play up?
<Kombucha Woman meme>
I hadn't given Bradish a second thought before now, but he's definitely heading to the watchlist after this write up. He may be a SP4-5, but he's relatively close and there's upside.

9 **Keegan Akin LHP**   OFP: 50   ETA: Debuted in 2020
Born: 04/01/95   Age: 26   Bats: L   Throws: L   Height: 6'0"   Weight: 225
Origin: Round 2, 2016 Draft (#54 overall)

The Report: The word "solid" takes a human form in Akin. The thick, stocky lefty has all the workings of a No. 5 starter, someone you can rely on, who has good, sometimes above-average stuff. He's regained full control and command of his low-to-mid-90s fastball, throwing it over 60 percent of the time. He holds velo well, touching as high as 96 this season, with the ability to overpower batters. His movements are clean and it's a standard, easily repeatable delivery with some deception. There's nothing particularly flashy about Akin, he gets into a rhythm and he gets the job done.

Development Track: Akin's developed his secondaries into genuine offerings, but the fastball is still the star of the show. While the change and slider appear average at best and still improving, they play up beside his fastball. The high-quality heater makes it easy for him to mix in the low-80s sinking changeup for swings and misses. His slurvy slider is the lesser of his off-speeds, but it induces weak contact and pop ups. He's still refining, but the changeup flashes above-average potential at times. It's a good sign. Like Kremer, Akin's bound to be part of the starting rotation next season and beyond.

Variance: Low. Akin was solid in his debut year, both as a starter and out of the bullpen. He's part of the O's future, one way or another.

Mark Barry's Fantasy Take: After a pair of middling relief appearances, Akin made six starts down the stretch for the O's and really was quite good, striking out a third of batters faced, with eight of his 10 earned runs coming from 3 2/3 innings in two ill-fated starts. The strikeouts are encouraging, and there's a good chance for positive regression thanks to a high BABIP and low strand rate. I am definitely talking myself into this system. Like Kremer, Akin might be a SP5/streamer-type, but the strikeouts lift the floor.

10 **Terrin Vavra SS**   OFP: 50   ETA: 2022
Born: 05/12/97   Age: 24   Bats: L   Throws: R   Height: 6'1"   Weight: 185
Origin: Round 3, 2018 Draft (#96 overall)

The Report: If Akin is solid made flesh, they may have re-used the cast on Vavra. He hit .380 his junior year at Minnesota with more walks than strikeouts. There was a small power spike which continued in the friendly confines of Asheville in 2019. He's the kind of college shortstop who ends up playing mostly second base—and he already had almost an even split between the two in A-ball. He'll hit enough and control the zone well enough that even low-double-digit home run totals should make him a solid enough major league hitter, something in the 5-10 percent better than average range. Nothing is going to stand out on the scout sheet, but he does everything well enough.

Development Track: Vavra was handled fairly conservatively by the Rockies, spending all of 2019 in the South Atlantic League despite being a relatively polished college bat. His power numbers will no longer get a boost from the Rockies' spate of bandboxes and/or high altitudes throughout their minor league system, but Vavra offers enough advanced offensive skills that you could start him at Double-A in 2021—I'm sure MLB will let us all know where that will be soon enough—without him missing a beat. He did miss a year though, so variance creeps in here like it does with most of the prospect population.

Variance: Medium. Vavra can hit and play both middle infield spots, so he's likely to carve out a major-league role of some sort. But if there is such a thing as an infield tweener, he might fall into that camp. I suppose I am obligated to mention there's an underlying skillset here that could yield more game power with a swing adjustment, but oh, that way madness lies for both Kings and prospect writers.

Mark Barry's Fantasy Take: Vavra put up some good numbers in Ashville last year, stealing 18 bases in just over 100 games. That's good! He also got caught nine times, however, which is definitely less, uh, good. Using a lazy, new-teammate comp, he could be the heir apparent for Hanser Alberto, in other words a guy who seems good, but in reality is just a multi-positional guy for deep-flexibility.

The Prospects You Meet Outside The Top Ten

Recent draftees with upside

Gunnar Henderson SS Born: 06/29/01 Age: 20 Bats: L Throws: R Height: 6'3" Weight: 195 Origin: Round 2, 2019 Draft (#42 overall)
Henderson was a tricky rank. He was badly overmatched at the alternate site, but he was also facing a lot of the arms above him on this list, as well as a bunch more close-to-ready backend starter types. And this was functionally his pro debut. He looked more like the draft report at instructs against age-appropriate competition, a projectable power bat that should land somewhere on the left side of the infield, likely at third base. There's more upside here than the back half or so of the Orioles Top 10, but the issues with bat control at the alternate site have us tempering expectations a tad for now.

Hudson Haskin Born: 12/31/98 Age: 22 Bats: R Throws: R Height: 6'2" Weight: 200 Origin: Round 2, 2020 Draft (#39 overall)
As Hunter Pence rides off into the sunset after announcing his retirement, we already have a candidate for his likely reincarnated baseball kindred spirit: meet Hudson Haskin. Setting aside their eerily similar names, their bodies and movements are also awkwardly similar in the way they shouldn't work at all and yet produce a ton offensively. Haskin is a plus runner with a good arm, albeit funky, with an innate ability to make contact despite a weird setup—tall and upright to begin with a very large stride that keeps him low through impact.

Coby Mayo Born: 12/10/01 Age: 19 Bats: R Throws: R Height: 6'5" Weight: 215 Origin: Round 4, 2020 Draft (#103 overall)
It may not have been their initial strategy, but Mayo became one of two Orioles draftees who benefited from the Kjerstad under-slot deal, signing for $1.75 million dollars ($1.18 million over the fourth round pick value). He's a mountain of a kid out of the south Florida prep scene who is a good athlete for his size. Some tinkering is needed to clean up the swing mechanics, however there is no shortage of bat-speed that can produce plenty of power.

Infielders you will see in the majors at some point

Adam Hall   SS   Born: 05/22/99   Age: 22   Bats: R   Throws: R   Height: 6'0"   Weight: 170   Origin: Round 2, 2017 Draft (#60 overall)
We've been talking a lot about teams telling us things while preparing for these lists. One way teams leaked information about whom they *really* like was alternate site assignments. The Orioles didn't invite Hall to the alternate site, even though they invited Henderson, who has a broadly similar profile as a prep infielder but is two years behind Hall developmentally. Based on 2019 looks, he's a hit-tool driven middle infield prospect who lacks significant power.

Jordan Westburg   Born: 02/18/99   Age: 22   Bats: R   Throws: R   Height: 6'3"   Weight: 203   Origin: Round CBA, 2020 Draft (#30 overall)
There were rumors that the subsequent target for the Orioles after Kjerstad in the compensation round—30th overall—would be prep pitcher Nick Bitsko. The Rays thwarted that plan six picks earlier, leaving Westburg as their consolation prize. A solid player with average tools across the board, and a projectable athletic body, Westburg had been trending upward before the season cancellation. He will need to show positional versatility to up his value, as well as try to tap into more power from his contact-oriented approach.

Starterish Upper Minors Types

Michael Baumann   RHP   Born: 09/10/95   Age: 25   Bats: R   Throws: R   Height: 6'4"   Weight: 225   Origin: Round 3, 2017 Draft (#98 overall)
Baumann has gone from Prospect Staff meme to pretty good prospect. He got a bump into last year's top ten as his secondaries improved around a solid-average fastball and the performance in Double-A backed it up. He's not all that different in quality of stuff or likely profile from the Akins and Bradishes or the world, but the former got the call over him, and the latter has a clear above-average secondary. It's fine margins at this part of the list though, and we wouldn't put you through the ringer if you prefer Baumann.

Kevin Smith   LHP   Born: 05/13/97   Age: 24   Bats: R   Throws: L   Height: 6'5"   Weight: 200   Origin: Round 7, 2018 Draft (#200 overall)
The Orioles got Smith from the Mets for Miguel Castro. The stuff is fringy—the fastball sits a tick either side of 90 and the slider flashes 50—but the extension, spin, and deception all help the arsenal play up. Whether it plays up enough to make him a back-end starter or merely a lefty middle reliever is yet to be seen.

Top Talents 25 and Under (as of 4/1/2021):

1. Adley Rutschman
2. Ryan Mountcastle

3. Grayson Rodriguez
4. Heston Kjerstad
5. DL Hall
6. Dean Kremer
7. Ryan McKenna
8. Kyle Bradish
9. Austin Hays
10. Terrin Vavra

This was, perhaps, the easiest 25-and-under list I'll ever have to deal with, outside of lists that exactly mirror the prospect list. Keegan Akin turns 26 on literally the day we set as the age cutoff for the list, so he drops off. The Orioles only have one eligible non-rookie on their 40-man, Austin Hays, and he just happens to slot in exactly where Akin does on the prospect list. Easy peasy, right?

Last year, Hays ranked 12th on the Baltimore prospect list. He was coming off a scorching September as Baltimore's regular center fielder, and frankly we took significant criticism for having him too low; we did not feel his level of offense was sustainable and weren't completely sold on his defense in center, either. A year later, I think *some* of our concerns have borne out. He was a slightly below-average hitter over the course of the season, and Baltimore chose to mostly play Cedric Mullins in center and Hays in a corner when Hays returned from a broken rib in September. He's neither as good as his 2019 cup of coffee suggested nor as bad as he was in 2017, and 2020's acceptable hitting and ability to play any outfield spot does represent a compromise between those outcomes.

Part 3: Featured Articles

Orioles All-Time Top 10 Players

by Rob Mains

POSITION PLAYERS

GEORGE SISLER, 1B (1915–1927)

The greatest Brown of all time, he hit .344/.384/.481 with the club. His .420 average in 1922 is the third-highest in history since the formation of the American League in 1901. He is also the franchise record-holder with 351 stolen bases, pacing the league four times. In the days before antibiotics, he missed the entire 1923 season with a severe sinus infection and wasn't the same hitter after that year (.782 OPS, three percent below the league average) as before (.914 OPS, 55 percent above average).

BOOG POWELL, 1B (1961–1974)

His image as big, slow slugger isn't fair. He was big (listed at 6'4", 230) and a slugger (his 303 homers as an Oriole trail only Ripken and Murray), but he was an okay fielder and he drew a lot of walks. His .822 OPS, adjusted for Memorial Stadium and the low-run environment in which he played; only Williams and Murray exceeded him. The O's recent struggles on the field and at the gate means shorter lines at his eponymous barbecue stand at Camden Yards.

EDDIE MURRAY, 1B (1977–1988, 1996)

The Orioles' run of infielders who never missed a game is remarkable. Excluding a hamstring pull that cost him 24 games in 1986, Murray missed only 37 games in his first dozen years with Baltimore. Adjusted for park and era, his .868 OPS is second in club history (minimum 1,000 games). He was a fine fielder as well, collecting three Gold Gloves, and one of the most productive switch-hitters of all time.

HARLOND CLIFT, 3B (1934–1943)

The Browns were dreadful when Clift played for them, with just one winning record and teams that went 43-111 and 46-108. He drew a ton of walks, putting him in the league's top ten for on base percentage five times. His .394 OBP trails only Williams' .403 in franchise history. He hit as many as 34 homers in a year, twice drove in 118, and he was a steady fielder. He just lacked a supporting cast.

BROOKS ROBINSON, 3B (1955–1977)

Another Baltimore legend, the all-time leader in every third-base fielding record (games, putouts, assists, double plays), Robinson was, like Ripken, remarkably durable. He's tied for record for most consecutive 140-game seasons, 16, and would've had 18 were it not for a two-month demotion to the minors in 1959 after a slow start to his second full season. His .267/.322/.401 career batting line is not impressive but much of it was accumulated during the low-offense 1960s and is also a testament to his glove—he was so talented he was able to play both before and after his offensive peak. He was MVP of the 1964 season and the 1970 World Series.

BOBBY WALLACE, SS (1902–1918)

He's believed to be the first infielder to field a ball and throw it while still moving, an action so standard that it makes you wonder how weird the game was in the 19th century. Wallace is remembered primarily for his glovework, but he was a slightly above-average hitter for the Deadball Era, batting .258/.326/.328 and stealing 138 bases for the Browns. He jumped from the National League to the American League after the 1901 season, signing a five-year, $32,500 contract (roughly $1.1 million today) that made him the highest-paid player in the sport.

MARK BELANGER, SS (1965–1981)

Yet another indestructible infielder, Belanger won eight Gold Gloves at shortstop, playing 144 or more games nine times. He played in a low-offense era, but there's no getting around the fact that he was a poor hitter (.227/.300/.280). He could draw walks and was good for a dozen or so stolen bases a year, which was enough to keep his superlative glove in the lineup.

CAL RIPKEN, SS (1981–2001)

With apologies to Yankee fans, the question isn't whether Derek Jeter was the greatest shortstop of all time, it's whether he ranks third behind Ripken and Honus Wagner or third behind Wagner and Ripken. Nineteen straight All-Star Games, two MVPs, never missed a game while playing the most demanding non-catcher position on the field. Historic not just for his work ethic, but for the way he redefined the possibilities of his position.

KEN WILLIAMS, OF (1918–1927)

His 1922 season, in which he hit .332/.413/.627 with 39 homers, 128 runs, 155 RBI, 37 stolen bases is forgotten now (partly because his teammate, Sisler, hit .420/.467/.594 and was MVP), but it made him the first player to hit 30 homers and steal 30 bases in a season, a standard nobody else reached until Willie Mays in 1956. He swung an enormous 40-ounce bat and used it to club 179 homers from 1920 to 1927, second in the league only to Babe Ruth.

PAUL BLAIR, OF (1964–1976)

Blair's career has an unfortunate parallel to Sisler's. On May 31, 1970, he was hit in the face by a pitch that broke his nose and caused serious eye injuries. To that point in his career, he had a .264/.319/.412 batting line, well above average in that era. For the remainder of his time in Baltimore, in a better offensive environment, he hit .247/.296/.369. Still, excluding the games he missed in 1970, he played Gold Glove defense (he won the trophy eight times) in center field in 140 or more games every year from 1967 to 1976.

PITCHERS

HARRY HOWELL, RHP (1904–1910)

A spitball-throwing Deadball Era pitcher, Howell's career 2.06 ERA is a franchise record that almost certainly will never be broken. As with many Browns pitchers, his 78-91 won-lost record is a function of the poor teams for which he pitched. The durable righty averaged 308 innings pitched over his first five years with St. Louis, likely leading to the shoulder injury that ended his career, at age 33, after one game in 1910.

JACK POWELL, RHP (1902–1903, 1905–1912)

By the time Powell jumped to the newborn Browns he was 29 and had been in the majors eight years. His record in St. Louis was 117-143, but that's a reflection of the teams for which he pitched. The Browns had a winning record in just two years when he was there and lost 100 games three times. His 2.63 ERA was better than that of his Deadball Era peers, and his 2229.2 innings pitched are, by a wide margin, the most by a Browns hurler. Traded to the Highlanders in return for Howell, but the Highlanders were good enough to sell him right back.

CARL WEILMAN, LHP (1912–1920)

From 1913 through 1916, Weilman pitched 1,122.1 innings, second in the American League to Walter Johnson. His 62-68 record was reflective of the Browns of that era; his 2.46 ERA was well below the league average. He developed tuberculosis early in the 1917 season, missing all but five games that year and all of 1918 battling it, losing a kidney to it. He was Comeback Player of the Year in 1919, when he went 10-6 with a 2.07 ERA over 20 starts, but he could pitch only one more season, succumbing to the disease in 1924.

URBAN SHOCKER, RHP (1918–1924)

No Browns pitcher won more games than Shocker's 126, nor had a better winning percentage than his .612. He holds the franchise single-season record for wins (27 in 1921) and innings (348 in 1922). In his Browns years he was in the top ten in the league for ERA, strikeouts, and wins five times. Most famous for being the best pitcher on the 1927 Yankees, he had been Yankees property to begin with but had been traded to the Browns because Miller Huggins had gotten a bad character report on him—errantly, as it turned out—and they had to reacquire him.

NED GARVER, RHP (1948–1952)

He pitched for some truly terrible teams. The Browns averaged 57-97 when he was there. Yet he went 20-12 for the 1951 Browns, who went 52-102, with a 3.73 ERA and a league-leading 24 complete games. He finished second in the MVP vote that year to Yogi Berra. His ERA was well blow average every year he was with the club. His 59-68 record as a Brown reflects on his teammates, not on him.

MILT PAPPAS, RHP (1957-1965)

Pappas was called up to the Orioles at the age of 18 after only three minor-league games and reeled off eight straight seasons in which he won at least 10 games and never had a losing record. He became the team's no. 1 starter, appearing in both 1962 All-Star Games and starting the 1965 contest. He threw hard but rarely walked anyone, leading the AL in strikeout-walk ratio in 1964. The Orioles were still shaking off their Browns legacy when he joined the club, winning only 74 games in 1958 and 1959, but had back-to-back third-place finishes in his last two years with the team. And he gave them the final push, going to Cincinnati in the trade that brought Frank Robinson to the Orioles.

DAVE McNALLY, LHP (1962–1974)

Outstanding curveballer McNally ranks second the Palmer in innings, starts, and wins in franchise history. He won 20 or more games four straight years, from 1968 to 1971, and was 7-4 with a 2.49 ERA in 14 postseason appearances. Traded to Montreal after the 1974 season, he refused to sign a contract. After the season, he and another pitcher, Andy Messersmith, filed a grievance, claiming that by not signing a contract, he was entitled to sign with any club for 1976. MLB claimed a right to renew contracts in perpetuity. An arbitrator ruled in favor of McNally, who'd retired by then, and Messersmith, and free agency was born.

JIM PALMER, RHP (1965–1984)

Palmer holds almost every significant franchise pitching record, and it's not close: He pitched nearly 1,300 more innings, started 137 more games, won 87 more decisions, and had almost 700 more strikeouts than anyone in Browns/ Orioles history. And he wasn't just a compiler of stats; he won the Cy Young Award in 1973, 1975, and 1976, and had an ERA below 3.00 nine of ten years from 1969 to 1978. After his retirement, he became a national and then a local broadcaster. Never led in strikeouts or strikeout rate, never in fewest walks per nine. He was just relentlessly effective.

MIKE FLANAGAN, LHP (1975–1987)

He was a stalwart for the great Orioles teams of the late 1970s and early 1980s, going 122-81 with a 3.73 ERA from 1977 to 1984. He won the Cy Young Award in 1979, when he went 23-9 with a 3.08 ERA for the American League champions. He's third in franchise history for innings and starts. After his career ended, he worked in the front office and as a broadcaster before his life sadly ended by suicide in 2011.

MIKE MUSSINA, RHP (1991–2000)

Mussina topped Palmer on two scores: His 147-81 record equates to a .645 winning percentage, and his 3.53 career ERA, much if it within the Steroid Era, was 30 percent better than average. He's first in club history in both categories among pitchers with at least 700 innings. He was in the top six in the league in ERA in seven of his eight full years in the Orioles' rotation. He could locate all four of his pitches, finishing among league leaders in strikeouts to walks in every one of his seasons in Baltimore.

A Taxonomy of 2020 Abnormalities

by Rob Mains

I'm going to start this with a trivia question. Trust me, it's relevant. Don't bother skipping to the end of the article to find the answer, it's not there.

Only five players have appeared in 140 or more games for 16 straight seasons. Who are they?

It's a trivia question starting off an essay, so you know how this works: Whatever you guessed, you're wrong. It's okay. As someone who purchased this book, chances are good that you're an educated baseball fan. But the circumstances behind 2020 force us to abandon, or at least seriously question, some of our favorite patterns and crutches for evaluating the game we love.

We just completed what was undoubtedly the strangest season in MLB history. No fans, geographically limited schedule, universal DH, seven-inning twin bills, runners on second in extra innings, a 16-team postseason, a club playing at a Triple-A stadium. Some of these changes will likely persist (sorry), but we've never had so many tweaks dumped on us all at once, at least not since they figured out how many balls were in a walk.

And the biggest, of course, was the 60-game season. The 19th century was dotted with teams that went bankrupt before the season ended, but the lone season with only 60 scheduled games was 1877. That year there were only six teams, the league rostered a total of 77 players (just 16 more than the 2020 Marlins), and batters called for pitches to be thrown high or low by the pitcher, who was 50 feet away. We can say the 2020 season was easily the shortest ever for recognizable baseball.

As such, it'll stand out. Few abbreviated seasons do. Just about everybody reading this knows the 1994 season ended after Seattle's Randy Johnson struck out Oakland's Ernie Young for the last out of the Mariners-A's game on August 11. The ensuing player strike wiped out the rest of the season and the postseason. Teams played only 112-117 games that year.

And many of you know that a strike in the middle of the 1981 season split the season in two, resulting in the only Division Series until 1995. Teams played only 103-111 games that year, the shortest regular season since 1885.

Those two seasons are memorable. So when we see that nobody drove in 100 runs in 1981, or that Greg Maddux was the only pitcher with 180 or more innings pitched in 1994, we think, "Of course. Strike year."

But we don't remember other short years. You might not recall that the 1994 strike spilled into the next year, chopping 18 games off the 1995 schedule. You might've read that the 1918 season, played during the last pandemic, ended after Labor Day due to the government's World War I "work or fight" order. A strike erased the first week and a half of the 1972 season, but that year's best known as the last time pitchers batted in the American League.

The point is, while we don't remember small changes to the schedule, we remember the big ones. The 1981 mid-season strike. The 1994 season- and Series-ending strike. And, of course, the pandemic-shortened 2020 season. We won't need a reminder why Marcell Ozuna's 18 homers were the fewest to lead the National League in a century. (Literally; Cy Williams led with 15 in 1920.)

Now, about that trivia question. The five players are Hank Aaron, Brooks Robinson, Pete Rose, Ichiro Suzuki, and Johnny Damon. The one nobody gets, of course, is Damon, and a lot of people miss Ichiro, whose last season of 140-plus games came garbed in the red-orange and ocean blue of Miami when he was 42. That's half of what makes it a good question. The other half is the two guys whom many think made the list but didn't. Lou Gehrig? His streak started in the Yankees' 42nd game of the 1925 season and lasted only 13 seasons after that. And everybody assumes Cal Ripken Jr. did it, having played 2,632 straight games over 17 seasons. But one of those 17 seasons was 1994, when the Orioles played only 112 games.

My point? *I just told you* everybody remembers the 1994 strike year, but everybody forgets it fell in the middle of Ripken's streak, separating the first twelve years from the last four. Just because we recall something doesn't mean it's always at the front of our minds.

Nobody is going to forget 2020, and baseball is obviously not the main reason. But there will come a time in the future when you're looking at a player's or a team's record, and there will be baffling numbers there for 2020, and you'll think, "I wonder what happened." (Not to mention the missing line for minor league players.) Just like you forgot that the 1994 strike limited Ripken to 112 games.

Try not to forget it, though. The 2020 season resulted in weird statistical results for several reasons.

There were only 60 games.
I know, duh. But that had impacts beyond counting stats like Ozuna's home run total or Yu Darvish and Shane Bieber leading the majors with eight wins. (I know, pitcher wins, but still.)

The 162-game season is the longest among major North American sports, and that duration gives us a gift. Over the course of a long season, small variations tend to even out. A player who has a ten-game hot streak will probably have a ten-game cold streak. A team that starts the year losing a bunch of close games will probably win a bunch of them. We get regression to the mean. Statistics stabilize.

Consider flipping a coin. Over the long run, we expect it to come up heads about half the time. But the fewer flips, the more variation there'll be. If you flip a coin six times, probability theory tells us you'll get at least two-third heads about 34 percent of the time. Flip it 30 times, your chance of two-thirds heads drops to five percent.

Or, relevant to this case, if you flip a coin 60 times, your chance of getting at least 36 heads—that's 60 percent—is 7.75 percent. Expand the coin-flipping to 162 times, and the chance of getting 60 percent heads drops to 0.73 percent.

In other words, the odds of an outcome that's 20 percent better (or worse) than expected is *more than ten times higher* when you flip your coin 60 times than when you do it 162 times. Call it small sample size, call lack of mean reversion, or call it luck not evening out, 162 is a lot more predictive than 60. You get much more variation over 60 games than over 162. Bieber's 1.63 ERA and 0.87 FIP aren't something we'd see over a full season, and neither is Javier Baéz's .203/.238/.360.

Some players' lines in 2020 look normal. Brian Anderson had an .811 OPS in 2019 and an .810 OPS in 2020. (He probably would have gotten that last point if he'd been given enough time.) But there are many like Bieber and Baéz, some of them from young players still establishing their talent levels. The answer to the question, "What went right or wrong for that guy in 2020?" is most likely "Nothing, it was just a 2020 thing."

Preseason training was abbreviated for hitters.

Every year, spring training drags. Players get tired of it, fans get tired of it, and you sure can tell sportswriters get tired of it. Yes, something to get everyone into shape is necessary, but does it really have to drag on for over a month? Can't we shorten it?

The 2020 season answered in the negative, at least for hitters. Warren Spahn is credited with saying that hitting is timing and pitching is upsetting timing. It appears nobody had his timing down after the abbreviated July summer camp. Through August 9—18 games into the season—MLB batters were hitting .230/.311/.395 with a .275 BABIP. That BABIP, had it held, would have been the lowest since 1968, the Year of the Pitcher. In recent years it's hovered around .300.

It didn't hold. Play returned to more normal levels the rest of the year: .249/.325/.425 with a .297 BABIP starting August 10. But batters whose play concentrated in those first two weeks wound up with ugly lines. Andrew

Benintendi went on the injured list with a season-ending rib cage strain on August 11. His final line: .103/.314/.128 in 14 games. Franchy Cordero went on the IL with a hamate bone fracture on August 9 and a .154/.185/.231 line. Even though he came back strong in a late September return, it was too late to repair his full-season numbers.

Preseason training was abbreviated for pitchers.

Every year, spring training drags. Players get tired of it, fans get tired of it … wait, I already said that. But the abbreviated preseason was tough on pitchers, too. As noted, they had the upper hand coming out of the gate. But then they lost that hand. And then their arms, too.

The 2020 season was spread over 67 days. During those 67 days, 237 pitchers hit the Injured List, compared to 135 in the first 67 days of 2019. A lot of those IL stints, though, were COVID-19-related. Still, over the first 67 days of the 2019 season, there were 72 pitchers on the IL with arm injuries. That figure jumped to 110 in 2020, a 53 percent increase.

There are a number of factors contributing to pitcher arm injuries, ranging from usage to velocity, but it appears that attenuated preseason training played a role. A lot of pitchers had super-short seasons due to arm woes. Corey Kluber, Roberto Osuna, and Shohei Ohtani combined for seven innings, none after August 8. All suffered arm injuries. We'll never know whether they'd have fared better with a longer preseason, but we can guess how they probably feel.

Everybody played.

Rosters were set to expand from 25 to 26 in 2020, so even if we'd had a normal season, we'd have likely seen 2019's record of 1,410 players on MLB rosters broken. But due to the pandemic, rosters started the year at 30 and were cut to only 28. Add multiple COVID-19 absences and the revolving door caused by poor starts by hitters and a rash of pitcher arm injuries, and 1,289 players appeared in MLB games in 2020. The comparable figure over the first 67 days of the 2019 season was 1,109. That 16 percent increase works out to an average of six more players per team in 2020 compared to a similar slice of 2019. A future look back at 2020 rosters will include a lot of unfamiliar names.

Plus became a minus.

In advanced metrics, we adjust batter and pitcher performance for park and league/era variations. A plus sign appended to the end of a measure means that it's adjusted for park and league. It's scaled to an average of 100, with higher figures above average and lower figures below average. (Similarly, a metric with a minus is also park- and league-adjusted and scaled to 100, with lower values better.) Here at BP, our advanced measure of offensive performance is DRC+. Baseball-Reference has OPS+ and FanGraphs has wRC+.

Using park and league adjustments, we can compare Dante Bichette's 1995 Steroid Era season at pre-humidor Coors Field (.340/.364/.620, 40 homers, 128 RBI, MVP runner-up) with Jim Wynn's 1968 Year of the Pitcher season at the cavernous Astrodome (.269/.376/.474, 26 homers, 67 RBI, no MVP votes). It's not close. DRC+, OPS+, and wRC+ all give the nod to Wynn, handily. This is a useful tool. As my Baseball Prospectus colleague Patrick Dubuque tweeted last fall, "Please note that when I ask how you are, I am already adjusting for era."

The 2020 season messes up plus (and minus) stats for two reasons. First, the park adjustment was based on only 30 home games instead of the usual 81. Everything noted above regarding the short season applies, literally doubly, to park effect calculations. DRC+ uses a single-season park factor. OPS+ uses a three-year average and wRC+ five years. The figure for 2020 is suspect.

Second, OPS+ and wRC+ adjust for league: American and National. (DRC+ adjusts for opponent, regardless of league.) While there were two leagues in 2020, they were an artificial construct. To reduce travel, teams played opponents geographically, not based on league. There weren't two leagues, American and National. There were three, Western, Central, and Eastern.

That makes a difference because teams in the same league played in different run-scoring environments. AL teams scored 4.58 runs per game, NL teams 4.71. That's a small difference. But teams in the East scored 0.21 more runs per game (4.95) than teams in the West (4.74), and they both scored a lot more than Central teams (4.25). Adjusting for league misses that difference, so this book will be safe in that regard, but other sources may be distorted somewhat.

Not every game was a "game."

In 2020, the rising tide of strikeouts was finally stemmed. Strikeouts per team per game fell from 8.8 in 2019 to 8.7 in 2020. That marked the first decline after 14 straight annual increases.

In 2020, the rising tide of strikeouts rose higher. Batters struck out in 23.4 percent of plate appearances compared to 23.0 percent in 2019. That marked the 15th straight annual increase.

Both are true statements.

Because of two rule changes—seven-inning doubleheaders and runners on second in extra innings—games in 2020 were unprecedented in their brevity. There were 37.0 plate appearances per game in 2020. The only years with fewer were 1904 and 1906-1909. The average game in 2020 entailed 8.61 innings pitched, the fewest since 1899.

So when you see any per-game stats for 2020, you need to increase them by 3 or 4 percent to get them on equal footing with recent years.

Or, better, just ignore them. Last year happened. There were major league games contested between major league teams. But when you're looking at those physical or electronic baseball cards, when you're weaving narratives over why this young player's inevitable rise to stardom fell apart or why that old veteran rekindled his magic, don't linger on the 2020 line. It was just too weird. ▪

Thanks to Lucas Apostoleris for research assistance.

—*Rob Mains is an author of Baseball Prospectus.*

Tranches of WAR

by Russell A. Carleton

We ask "replacement level" to be a lot of things. Sometimes contradictory things. Sometimes I wonder if we know what it even means anymore. The original idea was that it represented the level of production that a team could expect to get from "freely available talent", including bench players, minor leaguers, and waiver wire pickups. It created a common benchmark to compare everyone to, and for that reason, it represented an advancement well beyond what was available at the time. In fact, it created a language and a framework for evaluating players that was not just better but *entirely* different than what came before it.

But then we started mumbling in that language. The idea behind "wins above replacement" was one part sci-fi episode and one part mathematical exercise. Imagine that a player had disappeared before the season and suddenly, in an alternate timeline, his team would have had to replace him. The distance between him and that replacement line was his value. We need to talk about that alternate timeline.

Without getting too into 2:00 am "deep conversations" with extensive navel-gazing, it's worth thinking about why one player might not be playing, while another might.

- A player might not be playing because he has a short-term injury or his manager believes that he needs a day off.
- A player might not be playing because he has a longer-term injury that requires him to be on the injured list.

There's a difference here between these two situations. In particular, the first one generally *doesn't* involve a compensatory roster move, while the second one does. It's possible, though not guaranteed, that the person who will be replacing the injured/resting player would be the same in either case. That matters. Teams generally carry a spare part for all eight position players on the diamond, although in the era of a four-player bench, those spare parts usually are the backup plan for more than one spot.

A couple of years ago, I posed a hypothetical question. Suppose that a team had two players in its system fighting for a fourth outfielder spot. One of them was a league average hitter, but would be worth 20 runs below average if allowed to play center field for a full season. One of them was a perfectly average fielder, but would be 15 runs below average as a hitter, if allowed to play an entire season. Which of the two should the team roster? It's tempting to say the second one, as overall, he is the better player. That misses the point. A league average hitter on the bench isn't just a potential replacement for an injured outfielder. He might also pinch hit for the light-hitting shortstop in a key spot. You keep the average hitter on the roster, even though he isn't a hand-in-glove fit for one specific place on the field, because being a bench player is a different job description than being a long-term fill-in for someone. If you find yourself in need of a longer-term fill-in, you can bring the other guy up from AAA.

When we're determining the value of an everyday player though, if he had disappeared before the season and a team would have had to replace his production, they likely would have done it with a player who was a long-term fill-in type because they would have had to replace a guy who played everyday. Maybe that's the same guy that they would have rostered on their bench anyway, but we don't know. It gets to the query of what we hope to accomplish with WAR. Are we looking for an accurate modeling of reality or are we looking for a common baseline to compare everyone to? Both have their uses, but they are somewhat different questions.

Let's talk about another dichotomy.

- A player might not be playing because he isn't very good and is a bench-level player.
- A player might not be playing because there is another player on the team who has a situational advantage that makes him the better choice today. The classic case of this is a handedness platoon. On another day, he might be a better choice.

When we think about player usage, I think we're still stuck in the model that there are starters and there are scrubs. We have plenty of words for bench players or reserves or backups or utility guys. We do still have the word "platoon" in our collective vocabulary, but in the age of short benches, it's hard to construct one. It's always been hard to construct them. You have to find two players who hit with different hands, have skill sets that complement each other, and probably play the same position. In the era of the short bench, one of them had probably better double as a utility player in some way. Baseball has a two-tiered language geared toward the idea of regulars and reserves. The fact that it was so easy for me to find plenty of synonyms for "a player whose primary function is to come into a game to replace a regular player if he is injured or resting" should tell you something.

I'm always one to look for "unspoken words" in baseball. What is it called when someone is both half of a platoon and the utility infielder? That guy exists sometimes, but he reveals himself in that role—usually by accident. We don't have a word for that, and whenever I find myself saying "we don't have a word for that", I look for new opportunities. What do you call it, further, when the job of being the utility infielder is decentralized across the whole infield with occasional contributions from the left fielder? It's not even a "super-utility" player. What happens when you build your entire roster around the idea that everyone will be expected to be a triple major?

⚾   ⚾   ⚾

I think someone else beat me to this one, and on a grand scale. Platoons work because we know that hitters of the opposite hand to the pitcher get better results than hitters of the same hand, usually to the tune of about 20 points of OBP. If you want to express that in runs, it usually comes out to somewhere around 10 to 12 runs of linear weights value prorated across 650 PA. But hang on a second, now let's say that we have two players who might start today, both of roughly equal merit with the bat. One has a handedness advantage, but is the worse fielder of the two. In that case, as long as his "over the course of a season" projection as a fielder at whatever position you want to slot him into is less than a 10-run drop from the guy he might replace, then he's a better option today.

We're not used to thinking of utility players as bat-first options, who would play below-average defense at three different infield positions. That guy might hook on as a 2B/3B/LF type (Howie Kendrick, come on down!) but teams usually think to themselves that they need as their utility infielder someone who "can handle" shortstop, the toughest of the infield spots to play. If someone can do that *and* hit well, he's probably already starting somewhere, so he's not available as a utility infielder. It's easier for those glove guys to find a job. In a world where the replacement for a shortstop *has to be* the designated utility infielder, that makes sense.

But as we talked about last week, we're living in a different world. The rate at which a replacement for a regular starter turns out to be *another starter* shifting over to cover has gone way up over the last five years. There was always some of it in the game, but this has been a supernova of switcheroos. Now if your second baseman is capable of playing a decent shortstop, that 2B/3B/LF guy can swap in. He's not actually playing shortstop, and maybe the defense suffers from the switch, but if he's got enough of a bat, he might outhit those extra fielding miscues. And in doing so, he is effectively your backup shortstop.

Somewhere along the lines, teams got hip to the idea of multi-positional play from their regulars. I've written before about how you can't just put a player, however athletic, into a new position and expect much at first. The data tell us that. Eventually, players can learn to be multi-positionalists, but it takes time, roughly on the order of two months, before they're OK. But there's a hidden message in there. If you give a player some reps at a new spot, he's a reasonably gifted athlete and somewhat smart and willing to learn, he could probably pick it up enough to get to "good enough," and it doesn't take forever. You just have to be purposeful about it. Maybe you get to the point where you can start to say "he's still below average but we could move him there and get another bat into the lineup, and it's a net win."

Teams have started to build those extra lessons into their player development program. It used to be seen as a mark of weakness to be relegated to "utility player" because that meant that you were a bench player (all those synonyms above come with a side of stigma). Now, it's a way of building a team. If you get a few reps in the minors (where it doesn't count) at a spot, you'll have at least played the spot at game speed before. There are limits to how far you can push that. A slow-footed "he's out in left field because we don't have the DH" guy is never going to play short, but maybe your third baseman can try second base and not look like a total moose out there.

⚾   ⚾   ⚾

Back to WAR. I'd argue that the world of starters and scrubs is slowly disintegrating, for good cause. In the event that a regular starter really does go down with an injury–ostensibly, the alternate universe scenario that WAR is attempting to model–it makes the team a little more resilient to replacing him. And the good news is that you're more likely to be able to replace him with the best of the bench bunch, rather than the third-best guy, because the best guy doesn't have to be an exact positional match for the guy who got hurt. And that's what the manager would want to do. He'd want to replace that long-term production, not with an amalgam of everyone else who played that position, but with the best guy available from his reserves.

Now this is still WAR. We still want to retain the principle that we should be measuring a player, and not his teammates. We need some sort of common baseline, and despite what I just said, we'll still need some sort of amalgam. To construct that, I give to you the idea of the tranche. The word, if you've not heard it before, refers to a piece of a whole that is somehow segmented off. It's often used in finance to talk about layers of a financial instrument.

Here, I want you to consider that there are 30 starters at each of the seven non-battery positions (catchers should have their own WAR, since only a catcher can replace a catcher). We can identify them by playing time, and we can futz around with the definition a little bit if we need to. Next, among those who aren't in that starting pool, we identify the top tranche of the 30 best bench players, which I would again identify by playing time, and then the second and third and fourth and so on. If a player were to disappear, his manager would probably want to take a guy from that top tranche of the bench to replace him. In a world where even the starters can slide around the field, that becomes more feasible.

We can take a look at that top tranche and say "How many of them showed that they are able to play (first, second, etc.)?" and therefore could have directly substituted for the starter? How many of them could have been a direct substitute for our injured player? We don't know whether one of them would be on *a specific* team, but we can say that 40 percent of the time, a manager would have been able to draw from tranche 1 in filling the role, and 35 percent from tranche 2. But on tranche 1, we can also look at how many of those players played a position that could have then shifted and covered for that spot. We'd need some eligibility criteria for all of this (probably a minimum number of games played) but it would just be a matter of multiplication. Shortstop would be harder to fill, and managers would probably be dipping a little further down in the talent pool, and so replacement level would be lower, as it is now.

Doing some quick analysis, I found that the difference in just batting linear weights (haven't even gotten into running or fielding) between tranche 1 and tranche 2 in 2019 was about 6.5 runs, prorated across 650 PA. Between tranche 1 and tranche 3, it's 10.8 runs. The ability to shift those plate appearances up the ladder has some real value.

This part is important. We can also give credit to starters for the positions that they showed an ability to play, even if they didn't play them (this is the guy fully capable of playing center, but who's in a corner because the team already has a good center fielder) because he allows a team to carry a player who hits like a left fielder to functionally be the team's backup center fielder. He facilitates that movement upward among the tranches. We can start to appreciate the difference between a left fielder who would never be able to hack it in center (and the compensatory move that his team would have to make) and the left fielder who could do it, but just didn't have to very often.

Past that, you can continue to use whatever hitting and fielding and running metrics you like to determine a player's value, but when we get down to constructing that baseline, I'd argue we need a better conceptual and mathematical framework. It's going to require some more #GoryMath than we're used to, but I'd argue it's a better conceptualization of the way that MLB actually plays the game in 2020. If...y'know...MLB plays in 2020. If WAR is going to be our flagship statistic among the *acronymati*, then we need to acknowledge that it contains some old and starting-to-be-out-of-date assumptions about the game. We may need to tinker with it. Here's my idea for how. ▧

—*Russell A. Carleton is an author of Baseball Prospectus.*

Secondhand Sport

by Patrick Dubuque

Back before time stopped, I liked to go to thrift stores. Now that I'm older, I rarely ever buy anything—I don't need much in my life, now—but I still enjoy the old familiar circuit: check to see if there are baseball cards to write about, look for board or card games to play with the kids, scan for random ironic jerseys, hit the book section. It takes ten, maybe fifteen minutes. Thrift stores are the antithesis of modern online shopping, because you don't know what they have, and you don't even really know what you want. It's junk, literal junk, stuff other people thought was worthless. That's what makes it great.

In an idealized economy, thrift stores shouldn't exist. Everybody has a living wage, and every product has a durability that exactly matches its desired life; nothing should need to be given away, no one should need to be given to. But then, thrift stores shouldn't work on a customer experience level, either. You wouldn't think an ethos of "let's make everything disorganized and hard to find" would lead to customer satisfaction, but low-budget retailers like TJ Maxx and Ross thrive on this model. People like bargain hunting as much for the hunting as the bargain; it's part of the experience, spending time as if it's a wager. There's a thrill, occasionally, in inefficiency.

In sports, the modern overuse of the word "inefficiency" is a condemnation: It insinuates that there is *an* efficiency, a correct way to be found, and that all other ways are wrong ways. It's prevalent in baseball but hardly contained to it; the lifehack, the Silicon Valley disruption are other examples of productivity creep in our daily lives. Their modern success makes plenty of sense. Maximization of resources, after all, is its own puzzle, and an industry of European board games is founded upon it. It's fun to take a system and optimize it, unravel it like a sudoku puzzle. If there's only one kind of genius, after all, there's no way anyone can fail to appreciate it.

Baseball has been hacking away at these perceived inefficiencies since its inception: platoons, bullpens, farm systems were all installed to extract more out of the tools at hand. But it's been a particular badge of the sabermetric movement, from Ken Phelps and his All-Star Team to Ricardo Rincon and the darlings of *Moneyball*. It's business, but it's also an ethos: the idea that there's treasure among the trash, something we all failed to appreciate until someone brought it to light.

It's the myth that made Sidd Finch so enticing, that fuels so many "best shape" narratives and new pitch promises. We all, athletes and unathletic sportswriters, want to believe that there's genius trapped inside us, and that it's just a matter of puzzling out the combination to unlock it. That our art, our style is the next inefficiency, waiting for our own Billy Beane. It's why we root for underdogs, and why we're excited for the Mike Tauchmans and the Eurubiel Durazos, champions of skin-deep mediocrity.

Except we aren't anymore, really. The days of "Free X" have descended beyond the ring of irony and into obscurity. There are still Xs to be freed, or at least one X, duplicated endlessly: Mike Ford, Luke Voit, Max Muncy. The undervalued one-dimensional slugger demonstrated how the game hasn't quite culturally caught up to its logical extreme. But for those who don't fit the rather spacious mold, times are grimmer. As Rob Arthur revealed several months ago, there's been a marked increase in the number of sub-replacement relievers. It's the outcome of a greater number of teams forced to play out games without the talent to win them, but it's also emblematic of the modern tendency of teams to dispose of their disposable assets, burning through cost-controlled arms the way that man chopped down forests in *The Lorax*. Stuff just isn't built to outlive their original owners anymore.

It's unsurprising, given how well-mined the market for inefficiencies has been of late. The disciples of the early analytics departments, and the disciples of those, have proliferated the league, with only a few backwater holdouts. The league has grown smarter, but every team has learned the same lesson. In fact, the phenomenon creates a peculiar kind of feedback loop: As teams value a specific subset of players or skills, prospective athletes learn to increase their own marketability by conforming themselves to the demands of their prospective employers.

And that's tragic, in the way that the extinction of animals is tragic; a certain amount of biodiversity in baseball has been lost. Shortstops hit like outfielders. Pitchers don't hit at all. Only the catchers remain idiosyncratic, thanks to the defensive demands of their position; eventually they too will be required to produce like everyone else, or they'll meet the fate of their battery mates. A perfect economy requires perfect production.

I mentioned earlier that more and more, I leave thrift stores empty-handed. It is true that I am more discerning than in the past; my bookshelves are full, and there are more streaming films than I will ever be able to watch. But there are other factors at play.

Thrift stores are, in a way, the bond markets of retail. When the economy is rough and other retailers are struggling, more people look secondhand for their products. But as recently as last year, publications were noting a reversal of the trend: Companies like Goodwill and Savers were expanding despite a strong economy. Publications credited a heightened sense of environmentalism and a rejection of cutting-edge fashion as drivers behind the increase, though the more likely answer is the modern American economy hasn't showered its favors equally, particularly among the young.

But it is more than just the economy. Baseball and thrift stores share something else in common, evident in our current conversations about re-starting the sport: They live in the gray area between public service and private enterprise. Thrift stores provide affordable necessities to lower-class citizens, and collectibles and fashion for the middle-class. Because of the success of the latter, prices have gone up across the board. Especially in terms of clothing, the middle-class flight from fashion into vintage has instead carried the aftereffects of fashion, including its costs, into a territory where people just want clothes. But there's another factor in the rise of prices, in the form of the internet.

The Goodwills of the world have grown smarter, too, employing the internet to extract full value from their detritus. Ebay, similarly, has lost much of the charm it had as a new frontier around the turn of the century. Everything has a price point now; even individual taste is no match for the algorithm, because anything rare, no matter how niche its market, is a collectible to someone.

The internet has had the same effect on thrift stores that sabermetrics has had on baseball; its equivalent to OBP was the bar scanner. As detailed in Slate, the rise of second-party stores on eBay and Amazon birthed an entire industry of used-good salespeople, armed with PDAs and scanners, buying books for three dollars to sell online for five. The author, Michael Savitz, reports earning $60,000 by working nearly 80 hours a week; he makes it clear that this is not a vocation of his choosing. It's long hours, with no real creativity or individuality, skimming the cream off of a local establishment and flipping it to someone with a little more money on the other side of the country. And once the vocation exists, the obvious question arises: why wait to put the wares out on the shelves? Why allow value to exist at all?

Nothing is ruined. Thrift stores will continue to sell polo shirts and DVDs, and baseball will continue to exist and make or lose money, depending on who you believe. But as we continue to refine our knowledge, we lose something in the conquest for efficiency, a delight born out of the unknown. The problem isn't the efficiency itself; we can't blame the booksellers, or the people sweeping freeways to collect grams of platinum from damaged catalytic converters. The problem is a system that requires this sort of profit-skimming behavior in order to feed families (or, for corporations, maximize shareholder return).

In times like these, with the 2020 season on the brink and the collective bargaining agreement close behind, it can often feel like the current situation is untenable. It can't keep going like this, even if we don't know what to do about it. But as with thrift stores, there's an equally irresistible feeling that it *has* to keep going, that it would be unimaginable to not have this broken, amazing sport. Both industries exist on an invisible foundation of friction, of chaos and unpredictability, even as both see their foundations buffed down to a perfect, untouchable polish. But if COVID-19 and its financial ramifications do, as some have suggested, make it such that the baseball that returns is fundamentally different than the baseball that came before, perhaps this is the time to lean in, and change the game even more. Fix bunting. Make defense more difficult. Create viable, alternate strategies. Add some chaos back into baseball. It's fun when no one knows quite where things are. ▪

—Patrick Dubuque is an author of Baseball Prospectus.

Steve Dalkowski Dreaming

by Steven Goldman

We dream of being a pitcher, of starring in the major leagues. Depending on your age and your sense of historical perspective, you might imagine yourself as Walter Johnson, throwing harder than anyone else—hitting more batters than anyone else, too, but always feeling bad about it. You could picture yourself as a Tom Seaver or a David Cone, with all the stuff in the world but still being cerebral about it, thinking about so much more than burning 'em in there. There are so many models one could choose: You could be a Lefty Gomez, Jim Bouton, or Bill Lee, skilled, but not taking the whole thing too seriously, or a Lefty Grove, Bob Gibson, or Steve Carlton, powerful but treating each start like a mission to be survived instead of a game to be enjoyed.

Very few would dream of being Steve Dalkowski, the former Baltimore Orioles prospect who died of COVID-19 last week at the age of 80. Yet, there is something just as noble in Dalkowski's negative accomplishments—and accomplishments is what they are—as there is in the precision-engineered pitching of a Greg Maddux. You have to be very good to be that bad. Dalkowski had all of the stuff of the greatest pitchers but none of the command; his story is not one of failing to conquer his limitations, but striving against one of the cruelest hands that fate or genetics or personality can deal us: A desire to achieve great things which is almost but not quite matched by the ability to meet that goal.

As with Johnson, Grove, Bob Feller, and the rest of the hard-throwing pitchers who played before the advent of modern radar guns, we have to take the word of the players and coaches who saw Dalkowski pitch as to his velocity. He was a hard-drinking, maximum-effort pitcher who, if their memories are to be believed, consistently threw over 100 miles per hour. His was the Maltese Fastball, the stuff that dreams are made of. The problem is that velocity without command and control is still a good distance from utility. Dalkowski was the most effective towel you could design for a fish, the sleekest bathing suit intended to be worn by an astronaut, but that doesn't mean he wasn't beautiful: We can appreciate a journey even if it doesn't end at the intended destination.

Whether because of sloppy mechanics he couldn't calm, an inability to understand that a consistent 98 in the strike zone would likely be more effective than a consistent 110 out of it, or all that beer, Dalkowski could never make the adjustments that pitchers like Feller and Nolan Ryan made before him, possibly because he had so far to go: Feller, who never pitched in the minors, came up at 17 and spent three years walking almost seven batters per nine innings before settling in at 3.8 beginning when he was 20. Ryan started out walking over six batters per nine but gradually improved as his long career played out; for him to go from 6.2 walks per nine with the 1966 Greenville Mets to 3.7 with the 1989 Texas Rangers represents a 40 percent reduction. An equivalent improvement by Dalkowski would still have left him walking over 11 batters per nine innings.

Dalkowski was like *The Room* of pitchers, a player so bad he became good again. Cal Ripken, Sr., who both played with and managed Dalkowski, recalled in a 1979 *Sporting News* "where are they now" piece the occasion when the pitcher crossed up his catcher and his fastball, "hit the plate umpire smack in the mask. The mask broke all to pieces and the umpire wound up in the hospital for three days with a concussion. If they ever had a radar gun in those days, I'll bet Dalkowski would have been timed at 110 miles an hour."

Signed by the Orioles out of New Britain High in Connecticut in 1957, Dalkowski was sent to Kingsport in the Appalachian League, where he pitched 62 innings. He allowed only 22 hits in 62 innings, or 3.2 per nine, a number with no equivalent in major league history (though Aroldis Chapman came close in 2014), and also struck out 121 (17.6 per nine) and walked 129 (18.7). He was also charged with 39 wild pitches. That June, one of his fastballs clipped a Dodgers prospect named Bob Beavers and carried away part of his ear. "The first pitch was over the backstop, the second pitch was called a strike, I didn't think it was," Beavers said last year. "The third pitch hit me and knocked me out, so I don't remember much after that. I couldn't get in the sun for a while, and I never did play baseball again." Former minor leaguer Ron Shelton based the *Bull Durham* pitcher Nuke LaLoosh on Dalkowski. And yet, to see him as a figure of fun, an amusing loser, is to misunderstand something unique and strange.

Dalkowski kept on posting some of the strangest lines in baseball history. Pitching for the Stockton Ports of the Class C California League in 1960, he struck out 262 and walked 262 in 170 innings. Yet, he did improve, especially after pitching for Earl Weaver at Elmira in 1962. Weaver had previously had Dalkowski at Aberdeen in 1959, but wasn't ready to grapple with him then. This time he was. "I had grown more and more concerned about players with great physical abilities who could not learn to correct certain basic deficiencies no matter how much you instructed or drilled them," he related in his autobiography, *It's What You Learn After You Know It All That Counts*. He got permission from the Orioles to give all of his players the Stanford-Binet IQ test. "Dalkowski finished in the 1 percentile in his ability to understand facts. Steve, it was said to say, had the ability to do everything but learn." [sic]

IQ tests are problematic diagnostic tools, so take Weaver's estimate of Dalkowski's mental capabilities with a grain of salt. What's important is that even if he got to the right answer by way of the wrong reason, Weaver had learned something valuable. His insight was to stop asking Dalkowski to learn new pitches and just let him get by with the two that he had. Were Dalkowski a prospect today, that would have been a no-brainer: Can't develop a third pitch? The bullpen is right over there, sir. Player development wasn't like that then, but Weaver, temporarily Dalkowski's mentor, could let him work with what he had. According to Weaver, the pitcher responded: "In the final 57 innings he pitched that season Dalkowski gave up 1 earned run, struck out 110 batters, and walked only 11." It's not true—as per the *Elmira Star-Gazette*, as of late July, Dalkowski had walked 71 in 106 innings and finished with 114 in 160 innings, which means Dalkowski's control actually faded at the end of the season rather than improved—but that doesn't mean it didn't happen in some sense, just that it didn't happen that way. Again, it's the journey, not the destination, and his ERA was 3.04 so *something* had gone right.

Also along the way: The next spring, Orioles manager Billy Hitchcock was rooting for Dalkowski to make the team as a long-man—maybe Weaver had gotten through to him. There were things out of Weaver's control, like the universe's twisted sense of humor: that March, Dalkowski's elbow went "twang."

You sometimes read that it was the Orioles' insistence on Dalkowski learning the curve that did him in, but even if they hadn't learned their lesson, the injury was probably just a coincidence: Dalkowski had thrown an incredible number of pitches over the previous few years. Still, it testifies to the dangers of trying to get what you want and risking the loss of what you had. Dalkowski tried to come back, but the 110-mph stuff was gone. A pitcher with no control and no stuff is…a civilian. What followed were years of vagabond living, arrests for drunkenness. There were Alcoholics Anonymous meetings, assistance from baseball alumni associations, but none of it took. From the 1990s until the time of his passing he dwelt in an assisted living facility, suffering from alcohol-related dementia. He'd been a heavy drinker since his teenage years. As with all those pitches per game, there was a price to be paid. You make choices on the journey and some of them are irrevocable. It's like a fairy tale: "Bite of poison apple? Don't mind if I do."

In the aforementioned *Sporting News* profile, Chuck Stevens, the head of the Association of Professional Ballplayers of America, a ballplayer charity, said, "I've got nothing against drinking. I do it myself sometimes. But, I don't condone common drunkenness. We went through lots of heartache and many dollars, but Dalkowski didn't want to help himself and we weren't going to keep him drunk." The journey is *un*like a fairy tale: No one will come along and kiss it better, not if they're busy forming judgments.

In the end, we are left with a sort of philosophical chicken/egg conundrum: Is failing to meet your goals evidence of unfulfilled potential or the lack of it? Isn't what you did by definition what you were capable of doing? Or could you have broken through to something better with the right help, the right lucky break? These are unanswerable questions, and how we try to answer them may say more about us than about the people we're judging.

No pitcher ever has it easy. *All* pitchers must work hard. *All* pitchers must refine their craft. It's almost never just about *stuff*. Dalkowski dreaming is no insult to the great pitchers who made it; from Pete Alexander to Max Scherzer, they have all earned their way up. And yet, if it is true that we can only do as much as we can do, then the journey would be more of an adventure, the ultimate triumph or defeat more noble, if like Dalkowski we lacked 100 percent of the confidence, the command, the self-possession, the commitment, the resistance to making bad decisions that so many great players possess—to be gloriously human. Or, to put it more succinctly, it would be fun to be able to throw as hard as any person ever has. Even if just for a moment, and even if nothing more came of it than that, no one could say you hadn't lived life to the fullest. ▪

—*Steven Goldman is an author of Baseball Prospectus.*

A Reward For A Functioning Society

by Cory Frontin and Craig Goldstein

On July 5, Nationals reliever Sean Doolittle said in the middle of a press conference regarding the restart of Major League Baseball and what would later be known as summer camp, "sports are like the reward of a functioning society." This sentence was amidst a much longer, thoughtful reply about the societal and health conditions under which MLB players were being brought back. It's a very similar sentiment to one Jane McManus used on April 7, when she discussed the White House's meeting with sports commissioners. She said "sports are the effect of a functioning society—not the precursor."

Both versions of the same sentiment spoke to a laudable ideal in the context of a country that was not addressing a rampaging virus, and opting instead to bring sports back for the feeling of normalcy rather than the reality of it. "Priorities," as McManus said.

On Wednesday, the NBA's Milwaukee Bucks conducted a wildcat/political strike, refusing to come out for Game 5 of their playoff series against the Orlando Magic. The Magic refused to accept the forfeit, and shortly thereafter other playoff series were threatened by player strikes. Eventually the league moved to postpone that day's games, folding to players leveraging their united power.

The backdrop against which these actions took place was the shooting by police of Jacob Blake. Blake was shot in the back seven times by police, as he attempted to get into his vehicle. He managed to survive the assault, but is paralyzed from the waist down.

⚾   ⚾   ⚾

The step taken to walk out, first by the Milwaukee Bucks, then subsequently by other NBA, WNBA, and MLB teams, was a step toward upholding the virtue of the sentiment described by McManus and Doolittle. But that sentiment does not align with the broad history of sports in this and other countries, a history that contradicts the core of the idealistic statement.

119

Sports have been a significant part of American society for most of its existence, expanding in importance and influence in recent years. The idea that society was functioning in a way that was worthy of the reward of sports for most of that time is laughable. Much of America is not functioning and has not functioned for Black people, full stop. The oppressed people at the center of this political act by players, specifically Black players, in concert throughout the NBA and in fits and starts throughout Major League Baseball, have not known a society that functions for them rather than *because* of them.

Politics has been part of the sports landscape since the inception of sport, but for just about as long people have bemoaned its presence. Sports are to be an escape, it is said. An escape from what, though? A functioning society?

No, the presence of sports has never signified a cultural or political system that is on the up and up. Rather, the presence of sports *reflect and reinforce the society* that produces them.

ⓧ   ⓧ   ⓧ

The Negro Leagues were born out of societal dysfunction. The need for entirely separate leagues, composed of Black and Latino players barred from the Major Leagues because of racism? That is not a functioning society, and yet there were sports.

Even the integration of players from the Negro Leagues resulted in a transfer of power and wealth from Black-owned businesses and communities and into white ones, mirroring the dysfunction that had bled into every aspect of American society at the time. Japheth Knopp noted in the Spring 2016 Baseball Research Journal:

> The manner in which integration in baseball—and in American businesses generally—occurred was not the only model which was possible. It was likely not even the best approach available, but rather served the needs of those in already privileged positions who were able to control not only the manner in which desegregation occurred, but the public perception of it as well in order to exploit the situation for financial gain. Indeed, the very word integration may not be the most applicable in this context because what actually transpired was not so much the fair and equitable combination of two subcultures into one equal and more homogenous group, but rather the reluctant allowance—under certain preconditions—for African Americans to be assimilated into white society.

To understand the value of a movement, though, is not to understand how it is co-opted by ownership, but to know the people it brings together and what they demand. When Jackie Robinson—the player who demarcated the inevitability of the end of the Negro leagues—attended the March on Washington for Jobs and Freedom in 1963, he did so with his family and marched alongside the people. He stood alongside hundreds of thousands to fight for their common civil and labor rights. "The moral arc of the universe is long," many freedom fighters have echoed, "but it bends towards justice." The bend, it is less frequently said, happens when a great mass of people place the moral arc of the universe on their knee and apply force, as Jackie, his family, and thousands of others did that day.

⚾   ⚾   ⚾

Of course, taking the moral arc of the universe down from the mantle and bending it is not without risk. Perhaps the outsized influence of athletes is itself a mark of a dysfunctional society, but, nonetheless, hundreds of athletes woke up on Wednesday morning with the power to bring in millions of dollars in revenues. That very power, as we would come to find out, was matched with the equal and opposite power to *not* bring those revenues. That power, in hands ranging from the Milwaukee Bucks, to Kenny Smith in the *Inside the NBA* Studio, from the unexpected ally, Josh Hader, and his largely white teammates to the notably Black Seattle Mariners, would be exercised for a single demand: the end to state violence against Black people. Not unlike the March itself, it sat at the intersection of the civil rights of Black Americans and bold labor action. The March on Washington stood in the face of a false notion of integration—against an integration of extraction but not one of equality—and proposed something different. Just the same, the acts of solidarity of August 26, 2020 will be remembered in stark defiance of MLB's BLM-branded, but ultimately empty displays on opening weekend.

Bold defiance like this can never be without risk. By choosing to exercise this power, the Milwaukee Bucks took a risk. They risked vitriol and backlash from those they disagreed with. They risked fines or seeing their contracts voided, as a walkout like this is prohibited by their CBA. They risked forfeiting a playoff game, one that, as the No. 1 seed in the playoffs, they'd worked all year to attain. They didn't know how Orlando would respond. It wasn't clear that other teams throughout the league would follow suit in solidarity. And it wasn't known the league would accept these actions and moderately co-opt them by "postponing" games that would have featured no players.

If the league reschedules the games, some of the athletes' risk—their shared sacrifice—will be diminished, in retrospect. But they did not know any of that when they took that risk. And it is often left to athletes to take these risks when others in society won't, especially those of their same socioeconomic status and levels of influence.

It is athletes, specifically BIPOC athletes, that take them, though, because they live with the risk of being something other than white in this country every day. They are no strangers to the realities of police brutality. It seems incongruous then, to say that sports are a reward for a functioning society when we rely on athletes to lead us closer to being a functioning society. Luckily, our beloved athletes, WNBA players first and foremost among them, understand what sports truly are: a pipebender for the moral arc of the universe.

—Craig Goldstein is editor in chief of Baseball Prospectus. Cory Frontin is an author of Baseball Prospectus.

Index of Names

For the Joy of Keeping Score

THIRTY81 Project is an ongoing graphic design project focused on the ballparks of baseball. Since being established in 2013, scorecards have been a fundamental part of the effort. Each two-page card is uniquely ballpark-centric — there are 30 variants — and designed with both beginning and veteran scorekeepers in mind. Evolving over the years with suggestions from fans, broadcasters, and official scorers, the sheets are freely available to everyone as printable letter-size PDFs at the project webshop: www.THIRTY81Project.com

Download, Print, Score, Repeat ...

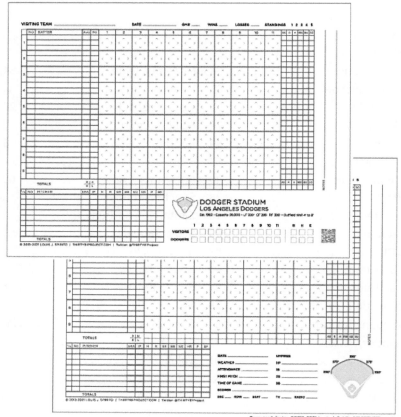

Scorecard design ©2013-2021 Louis J. Spirito | THIRTY81Project